P9-DDY-119

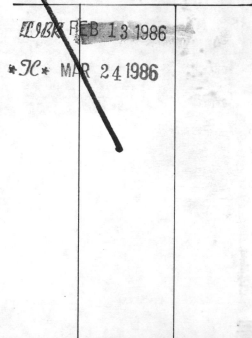

This BOOK may be kept out THREE WEEKS ONLY, and is subject to a fine of TEN CENTS a day thereafter. It is due on the day indicated below

LIBR FEB 13 1986

JC MAR 24 1986

The Iranian Rescue Mission

The Iranian Rescue Mission

WHY IT FAILED

E
183.8
.I 55
R 93
1985

By Paul B. Ryan

Naval Institute Press
Annapolis, Maryland

Copyright © 1985
by the United States Naval Institute
Annapolis, Maryland

All rights reserved.
No part of this book may be
reproduced without written permission
from the publisher.

Library of Congress Cataloging in Publication Data

Ryan, Paul B.
    The Iranian rescue mission.

    Bibliography: p.
    Includes index.
    1. Iran Hostage Crisis, 1979–1981.   2. United States—
Armed Forces—Search and rescue operations—History—
20th century.   3. United States—Foreign relations—
Iran.   4. Hostages—Iran.   5. Hostages—United States.
6. Iran—Foreign relations—United States.   I. Title.
E183.8.I55R93   1985   955'.054   85–7310
ISBN 0–87021–321–0

Printed in the United States of America

THOMAS COOPER LIBRARY
UNIVERSITY OF SOUTH CAROLINA
COLUMBIA, S. C. 29208

To the gallant eight
who gave their lives at Desert One

Wars may cease but the need for heroism shall not
depart from the earth, while man remains man and
evil exists to be redressed.

Mahan, *Life of Nelson*, 1897

Contents

Acknowledgments

The aborted rescue of American hostages at Tehran in April 1980 produced a torrent of news stories, explanations, and hindsight criticism. They touched on such themes as military tactics, diplomacy, military technology, and civilian direction of combat operations.

In this account, I have tried to draw together, within the limits imposed by security, all significant elements of the tragic episode that ended at Desert One. Because the official records pertaining to the planning and execution of the rescue remain classified, the complete story may remain unknown for years to come.

Yet much has been uncovered, thanks to the sanitized report of the Review Board headed by Admiral James L. Holloway III. Personal accounts of participants, which cannot be verified from the archives, have added to the store of information.

When the disaster is viewed from the evidence presently available, the facts suggest that the operation exposed serious deficiencies in the military decision-making system that may require substantial changes.

My thanks are extended to the following for information of various kinds: Dr. Dean C. Allard, Archivist of the U.S. Naval Historical Center, Washington, D.C.; Jane E. Blomberg, British Broadcasting Corporation, New York, N.Y.; Robert A. Carlyle, Office of Information, Navy Department, Washington, D.C.; Rear Admiral David M. Cooney, USN, chief of information, Navy Department, Washington, D.C.; Fynnette Eaton, National Archives and Record Service, Washington, D.C.; Jean Ineson Ebbert; Captain Leigh Ebbert, USN (Ret); Ellen Garrison, archivist, Georgia State University, Atlanta, GA; Dr. James L. George, Department of State, Washington, D.C.; Charles Haberlein, U.S. Naval Historical Center, Washington, D.C.; Robert Hartmann, Washington, D.C.; Patricia Hill, Georgia State University, Atlanta, GA; Barbara Lynch, Navy Department Library, Washington, D.C.; Dr. John T. Mason, U.S. Naval Institute, Annapolis, MD; Lieutenant Colonel H. E. Robertson, USAF, Office of Chairman, Joint Chiefs of Staff, Washington, D.C.; Colonel Thomas C. Shaefer, USAF (Ret); Jim Shults, editor, *Gung-Ho*; Brigadier General Edwin H. Simmons, director, Marine Corps History and Museums, Washington, D.C.; Bettie Sprigg, Office of Defense Information, the Pentagon, Washington, D.C.; Admiral Stansfield Turner, USN (Ret); Mary A. Terry, Marine Corps Headquarters, Washington, D.C.; Frank Uhlig, Naval War College, Newport, RI; Anna Urband, Office of Information, Navy Department, Washington, D.C.; Henry Vadnais, head, Curator Branch, U.S. Naval Historical Center, Washington, D.C.

The following were most helpful in furnishing technical information on maritime, aviation, and communications matters: Vice Admiral E. P. Aurand, USN (Ret); Captain Phil H. Bucklew, USN (Ret); Robert G. H. Carroll III, Sikorsky Division, United Aircraft, Stratford, CT; Rear Admiral C. A. Hill, USN (Ret), Association of Naval Aviation, Washington, D.C.; Captain Andrew C. A. Jampoler, USN, Naval Air Station, Moffett Field, CA; Rear Admiral R. E. Kirksey, USN, Navy Department, Washington, D.C.; Captain

Charles A. Leader, USMC; Dr. Edward Teller, Hoover Institution, Stanford, CA; Ensign Marcia Van Wye, USN, Staff, Commander Patrol Wings, Pacific Fleet.

I am also deeply indebted to Dr. Stephen Jurika, Captain John V. Noel, USN (Rct), Dr. Richard Staar, and Vice Admiral James B. Stockdale, USN (Ret). They graciously agreed to review the manuscript and, without assuming any responsibility, provided valuable comments. I must record my special thanks to Admiral James L. Holloway III for furnishing an unclassified version of his group's report and for granting me a lengthy interview.

The staff of the Hoover Institution, Stanford University, were unfailingly helpful, as was Betty J. Herring who typed the manuscript and was an able editing assistant.

Thomas F. Epley, director of the Naval Institute Press, Richard R. Hobbs, acquisitions editor, and Cynthia Barry, book editor, gave unstintingly in preparing the manuscript for publication.

The Iranian Rescue Mission

1

Background to a Debacle

An Ill-Starred Operation

In the early dawn of 24 April 1980, in the Iranian desert, a group of some 130 Army Green Berets, Rangers, drivers, and Iranian translators plus some 50 pilots and air crewmen were forced to abort the rescue of 53 Americans held hostage in Tehran.[1] The commander on the scene made the decision reluctantly after three of his eight helicopters, for various reasons, were not able to complete the mission. Worse yet, as the evacuation got under way, a helicopter, maneuvering close to the ground, sliced into a large transport plane laden with fuel and ammunition. Both aircraft burst into flames, and eight men died. The remainder flew to safety, leaving behind five helicopters, weapons, communication equipment, valuable secret documents, and maps, all of which, presumably, would be shortly demolished by U.S. attack aircraft. As the senior Green Beret later reported, President Jimmy Carter would not allow the strike, presumably because it would have jeopardized the lives of about 40 Iranians who had been captured in a bus at the landing site.

The rescue plan called for six giant C-130 transport

planes to lift the men, equipment, and helicopter fuel from an Egyptian air base to an island airfield off Oman for a refueling stop. The planes would then fly to a secret landing strip in Iran, designated "Desert One," 265 nautical miles from Tehran. There they would be joined by eight Sea Stallion helicopters launched three hours earlier from the aircraft carrier *Nimitz*, on station in the Arabian Sea. The rescue force would then transfer to the helicopters and fly to Desert Two, a remote mountain hideaway 50 miles from Tehran. The helicopters would be concealed at a site about 15 miles away. That evening the raiders would be clandestinely driven in vans and trucks to Tehran. About 11 P.M. that night, they would storm the compound, immobilize the guards, and free the hostages.[2]

While the main group overran the embassy, a smaller band would break into the Foreign Affairs Ministry and rescue the U.S. chargé d'affaires, Bruce Laingen, and two other Americans. Some forty minutes after the initial break-in, the raiders and hostages would board waiting helicopters at the embassy compound or, if the compound was not usable, at a nearby soccer stadium. If the Delta team, as the rescue group was called, found its way blocked by Iranian mobs, then two C-130 gunships, circling overhead, would immobilize the crowd with gatling guns, which fire 17,000 rounds per minute. Meanwhile, about eighty Rangers would be airlifted from Qena, Egypt, to an isolated desert airstrip at Manzariyeh, thirty-five miles south of Tehran. They would land, seal off the field, and await the arrival of C-141 Starlifters. Next, the helicopters would arrive and discharge their passengers. The helicopters would then be destroyed by their crews. A C-130 gunship would orbit overhead to cover the evacuation. Finally, the loaded transports would take off, presumably to return to Qena and freedom.

That was the plan. Even before the mission was half completed, it ended tragically, and the Carter administration faced a cascade of criticism for what many considered a military blunder.[3]

Who Was at Fault?

The disaster immediately raised doubts about U.S. military capabilities and the state of readiness of the armed forces. Furthermore, the mechanical failure of three helicopters suggested that Americans had lost their technological edge. The seeming ineptness of the operation stood in stark contrast with successful rescue operations conducted with little loss of life by the Israelis at Entebbe and by the West Germans at Mogadishu. Although U.S. forces had excelled in a difficult mission off the Cambodian coast when they had rescued forty crew members and recovered the U.S. merchant ship *Mayaguez*, that had been back in 1975 and had cost forty-one lives. Granted the Tehran rescue attempt was directed against a target some six thousand miles away, but the other operations had also been conducted thousands of miles from their respective bases, and with dispatch. What went wrong in the Tehran raid, Americans asked.[4]

Shortly after the disaster President Jimmy Carter, in a setting reminiscent of President John Kennedy explaining the Bay of Pigs fiasco, appeared on national television. To a shocked audience, a somber Carter expressed his deep regret over the loss of the eight servicemen, emphasizing that they had died carrying out a "humanitarian mission" designed to safeguard American lives. Mechanical breakdowns had compelled him to cancel the mission before it had been completed.[5] He maintained that this "difficult and dangerous" operation had had an "excellent chance of success," and he acknowledged that the responsibility for the failure was fully his own.

The president's ready assumption of blame did not prevent a barrage of censure against those who were responsible for this disastrous operation. To some analysts and journalists, the episode demonstrated that the Defense Department was incapable of mounting a combined assault, especially in distant territory. On Capitol Hill, the Senate Armed Services Committee met in secret to grill the military participants.

Critics familiar with commando raids charged that the Pentagon, the White House, and the Central Intelligence Agency should have known that a primary rule for a covert operation is "Get in fast and get out fast." The rescue plan, which had a duration of almost two days in hostile territory, obviously did not meet that maxim.

Politically, the Carter administration could not afford any bad publicity generated by a congressional probe. The president's ratings in public opinion polls were low, while those of Ronald Reagan, his chief Republican rival for the presidency, were on the rise. If an investigation revealed evidence of flaws in the planning process, for which Carter would be held accountable, his ratings would decline even more. For reasons of state, the White House justifiably was concerned that sensitive matters might be exposed involving covert assistance furnished by Egypt, which had supplied the staging base, and by Oman, which had helped in refueling. Thus, the administration arranged for an informal committee to examine military aspects only.[6]

Customarily, in the wake of a military disaster, the Defense Department initiates an inquiry by naming a board of investigation. In this case, however, the department chose to avoid a judicial board with power vested by military law. Instead, General David Jones, chairman of the Joint Chiefs of Staff, named a "review group." Furthermore, the chairman of the group, Admiral James L. Holloway III, and the five members, all of whom were of flag or general officer rank, were instructed to identify only those "lessons learned" in a military sense.[7]

Because of its narrow mandate, the Holloway panel was required to leave many questions unanswered. Although a sanitized version of its report was released in August 1980, as of 1985, the transcripts of individuals who were questioned by the Holloway panel remain classified, as do all documents relating to the planning, training, and actual assault operation. My efforts to obtain such information were refused by government officials and military officers on grounds of national security. For similar reasons none of the assault force, save for a few senior officers, was ever officially identified as a participant. In the belief that the identity of individuals who might be involved in future special operations should be concealed, the Carter administration initially ordered the Pentagon not to release standard public-relations photographs or boiler-plate biographical sketches of officers. But by 1984 some had come to light.

Admiral Holloway has told me that, despite the clampdown on information, his sanitized report contains most of the substance of the secret version. Other facts were revealed by Colonel Charlie A. Beckwith, who led the assault team and later spoke to reporters at two Pentagon press conferences, the only task force officer to do so. A colorful combat soldier, he shed more light on the tragedy when his reminiscences were published in November 1983 in *Delta Force*, composed in collaboration with a professional writer. To date, Beckwith is the only military officer involved in the mission to have written at length on the disaster.

Zbigniew Brzezinski, Carter's national security adviser and a key man in the episode, published his version of the operation in a long article in the *New York Times Magazine* and in his memoirs.[8] Other accounts appear in memoirs published by Carter and Hamilton Jordan. Secretary of State Cyrus Vance, the dissenter to the operation, resigned shortly after the raid. His memoir, *Hard Choices*, was published in 1983.[9] The published material, while helpful and to an extent revealing, leaves gaps. We do not yet have all the evidence at hand by which to weigh the alternatives that were open to Carter and to judge whether he could have avoided the calamity entirely. We do, however, have enough material now in the public record to describe the military operation itself and to assess its strengths and weaknesses.

The United States and Revolutionary Iran

A former one-term governor of Georgia, President Carter had no experience in foreign affairs or the use of force in diplomacy. Not surprisingly, his competence in international crises was severely tested when he found himself caught up in a Middle East revolution led by a fanatical mullah, the Ayotollah Ruhollah Khomeini.[10]

Tension between the United States and Iran reached a near breaking point in 1978. At the time, oil-rich Iran, a military ally, was split by a revolution engineered by Moslem fundamentalists against the Shah, Mohammed Reza Pahlavi. The revolt immediately endangered the status of Iran as a bulwark in Washington's strategy to block possible Soviet intrusion into the Middle East.

If the Iranians were rebelling against the brutality of SAVAK, the Shah's secret police, it is also true that the upheaval stemmed from a rejection of Western materialism and moral values. "Foreign decadence" was symbolized by the presence of costly U.S. weaponry, Cadillacs, and revealing feminine fashions, the latter soon to be replaced by robes and the chador, a decorous veil. The alleged debasement of Iranian life and the corruption of its people could be traced in large part to the "American Satan," according to the exiled Khomeini from his refuge in France.

The Carter administration either ignored or was ignorant of Iran's long tradition of Islamic puritanism. Few in the United States sensed that the Shah's goal of Westernizing his nation was about to be overturned by an unstable, monomaniacal septuagenarian leading a nation whose history was marked by spells of asceticism and xenophobia.[11]

On 16 January 1979, with his army disintegrating, the Shah fled to Egypt, leaving the nation under the uncertain control of Prime Minister Shahpour Bakhtiar. Returning in triumph from France on 1 February, Khomeini was welcomed by two million cheering people. The next day a mass exodus of American residents began. In all, forty-five thousand U.S. citizens were evacuated, many of them having been employed by American firms engaged in the Shah's construction projects. Despite portents of violence evident from Iranian press accounts of the "Great Satan" (Carter) and from mobs on the streets shouting "Death to the Americans," the Carter administration continued to believe that it could come to an accommodation with the new government. Accordingly, although most were called home, some seventy-five Foreign Service personnel were retained at their posts.[12]

With law and order crumbling in Tehran, rumors spread that the U.S. Embassy was harboring SAVAK officers in the compound. On 14 February 1979, rampaging revolutionaries, some of them armed, broke into the embassy, seized about seventy Americans, and demanded that Washington arrange for the return of the Shah for punishment—probably execution. During the melee, one Iranian employee was killed and two Marine guards were wounded. In the streets of Tehran, gangs looted stores and residences. Fortunately, the new government quickly persuaded the rioters to release the Americans and clear out of the embassy. The affair was an unmistakable signal that the safety of foreign diplomats, particularly those of the United States, was in jeopardy.

Carter, in his memoir, devotes two paragraphs to the episode. He recalls that during this time, the "most disastrous incidents were the capture of American personnel" who were released after "a frightening interval of several days." He then goes on to write that "despite the turmoil [he] was reasonably pleased with the attitude of the Iranian government under [Prime Minister] Bazargan."[13]

During the weeks following the temporary taking of the embassy, Khomeini continued to vilify the United States. Although Washington had its eyes on Iran's soil, he told the people, the nation would triumph over "satanical forces." Other speakers broadcast their warnings that the United States, as the "chief enemy," would not stop at the massacre of millions of people. In April 1979, before a crowd of 100,000, Khomeini accused the United States of creating disunity in Iran by setting in motion satanic plans. In May, a crowd of 150,000 marched to the embassy shouting "Death to Carter!"

Carter disregarded such denunciations, failing to appreciate the extent of the violent hatred so openly expressed by

Khomeini's multitudes. The president did, however, urge the several thousand Americans who still worked in Iran to leave. In the following year, all but about two hundred took the advice, and, as we shall see, it was this group that unwittingly became an awkward element in any plan to rescue the hostages.[14]

The Broken Promise of Protection

The U.S. government did not know that the Shah suffered from lymphoma, a virulent form of cancer which prompted him to seek medical aid in the United States. Ignoring an earlier report from the U.S. Embassy predicting a violent reaction in Iran if the Shah were admitted, the president, on 20 October 1979, approved the royal visit to the New York Hospital-Cornell Medical Center, because it had a team of experts and state-of-the-art radiation equipment. Other countries possessed hospitals that might have treated the Shah's ailments, but for political reasons, he was not welcomed or else he chose not to accept their offers of assistance. At the U.S. hospital he had a gall bladder operation and received radiation therapy. The disease had progressed too far, however, and the Shah died in Egypt ten months later.

With regard to the Shah's visit to the United States, Carter points out in his book, *Keeping Faith*, that high Iranian officials had given a guarantee of protection for U.S. citizens in Iran during the Shah's stay in New York. No one seemed disturbed that the Iranian government took no steps to place an armed guard around the embassy. And Washington did not direct the virtually unprotected embassy staff to destroy all classified documents in its files.[15]

Although by November 1979 President Carter had reduced the embassy staff substantially, he had declined to recall all personnel, in spite of the signs of impending chaos. He believed that by leaving a limited embassy staff in place he would shore up confidence in the prime minister.[16] Bakhtiar seemed sympathetic to U.S. interests but was walking a tightrope, trying to placate Khomeini while, at the same time, observing the niceties of diplomatic protocol. Carter was convinced that the small embassy staff would be safe because, according to Vance, security had been strengthened to permit the staff to hold out against a mob for two or three hours. During this time, the White House assumed, Iranian troops would arrive and restore order.

By clinging to the idea that the United States could deal with Iran, as Vance put it, "on the basis of friendship and mutual respect," the administration put too much faith in Iran's government to act in accord with the norms of diplomacy. When Premier Mehdi Bazargan stated on 21 October 1979 that Iran would guarantee the protection of the embassy, Carter and his advisors, to their later regret, believed him. The White House had underestimated the rabid anti-Americanism of the mullah-inspired Iranians, and on 4 November 1979, the embassy was captured by a mob. The takeover lasted 444 days.

Iran Flouts International Law

The assault on the embassy followed various outrages committed in recent years by small nations who had discovered that they could commit transgressions that in the past would have provoked the United States into a swift display of force. The list includes the capture of the tiny USS *Pueblo* by the North Korean navy in 1968; attacks on U.S. diplomats at Khartoum in 1973, Cyprus in 1974, and Malaya in 1975; and the murder of U.S. Ambassador Adolph Dubs at Kabul in February 1979. But the Iranian behavior plumbed new depths of international lawlessness, and on 21 November 1979 an anti-American mob in Islamabad, Pakistan, followed its example, attacking the U.S. Embassy and killing two U.S. servicemen.[17]

Governments very seldom detain foreign diplomatic personnel. First, a nation so tempted may invite harsh retaliation by military forces; second, diplomats abroad are presumed to be protected by the Convention on Diplomatic Relations of 1961, signed in Vienna by 82 states, including

Iran. The 1961 Convention extended the field of diplomatic protocol well beyond that of the Reglement (Rules or Regulations) of Vienna, compiled in 1815 at the close of the Napoleonic Wars. The Convention of 1961 noted that nations, since ancient times, have recognized the special status of diplomats and the immunities granted them. The document expressly provides for the inviolability of embassy staff, premises, and archives.[18]

Until the 1960s, violations of diplomatic immunity were relatively rare. One such incident took place in 1900 when Chinese revolutionaries, known as the Boxers, attacked embassies in Peking but were thrown back by foreign troops. An eighteen-thousand-man international rescue force was rushed from warships at the Taku Bar on the China Sea to Tientsin and thence to Peking. But a half-century later times had changed. In the post–World War II era of global egalitarianism, world powers seemingly became resigned to the fact that many small countries showed little respect for international law. The reluctance of the United States, and also other major nations, to use force against these international troublemakers led certain nations to believe that they could offend the larger nations, such as the United States, with impunity. Their growing contempt for established custom and international protocol was expressed in acts of terrorism by quasi-military forces, assassins, or even organized mobs, acting as agents for foreign regimes or governments. Such were the international influences bearing on Tehran prior to November 1979 as the president tried to come to terms with Khomeini.[19]

Carter's constant concern was for the safety of the prisoners. He worried about them during his early-morning walks, and he passed sleepless nights thinking of ways to rescue them without sacrificing honor and security. When he met with the hostages' families, he shared their feelings of grief and alarm. On learning of ill-treatment inflicted on the prisoners, he was sickened and alarmed because they sometimes seemed like part of his own family. More than anything else, he recalled, he wanted the prisoners to be free.[20]

Some critics believed that the president envisioned the hostages' fate in far too subjective terms. Allegedly, in March 1980, State Department specialists on Iran proposed to Secretary Vance that Carter should cease his emotional emphasis on the plight of the hostages. Instead, they suggested, he should downplay the crisis and tell Iran that if any harm came to the hostages, the United States would retaliate very quickly. Nothing came of the proposal, however, because the president had already decided on the military raid.[21]

No one except Cyrus Vance argued that the United States should not attempt to rescue the hostages because they were in no physical danger. Vance believed that Khomeini was using the hostages to consolidate his control of the revolution. To kill them would end their usefulness. Vance also opposed the use of military force because it would risk the lives of hostages and jeopardize U.S. interests in the Persian Gulf. He believed that a military strike would unite the Moslem world against the United States and its allies. Finally, he pointed to the precedent set by the USS *Pueblo* incident of 1968. The *Pueblo* officers and crew were imprisoned for a year by North Korea and were set free after negotiations because they had lost their propaganda value for their captors. Similarly, Vance maintained, the Tehran hostages would be released once Khomeini realized that they had become a political liability rather than an asset.

Others agreed with Vance, pointing out that the plight of the hostages, while dreary and odious, did not approach the barbaric treatment of American POWs in Hanoi who suffered torture, starvation, and solitary confinement. One who was qualified to comment on hostage–POW differences was Vice Admiral James B. Stockdale. A naval aviator, he had spent eight years as a prisoner of war in North Vietnam, and he believed that, in regard to Iran, Washington should have taken a harder line. The Iranian experience bore a distinct relationship to the Hanoi POW era, said Stockdale, who concluded that a U.S. policy of "being nice" to the enemy so that he will be "nice to your captives" was false and futile. In short,

Carter's reluctance to threaten force, coupled with television's portrayal of street-theater as played in Tehran, encouraged Khomeini to continue to blackmail the United States by manipulating the hostages.[22]

Brzezinski and the Rescue Plan

The ordeal of the hostages began 4 November 1979, a rainy Sunday, when five hundred militant "students," with Khomeini's blessing, invaded the embassy compound, seizing some sixty Americans. American television screens were filled with noisy street mobs shouting anti-U.S. slogans and demanding the return of the Shah. Two days later, Brzezinski, speaking for President Carter, telephoned Defense Secretary Harold Brown and "instructed him to have the Joint Chiefs of Staff develop a plan" to free the prisoners. A rescue mission, Brzezinski later wrote, was a matter of honor as well as "a moral and political obligation to the prisoners." As events turned out, Carter approved the idea of the raid without fully understanding if it were suitable for the intended purpose— that of rescuing the hostages unharmed. He appointed Brzezinski to coordinate and oversee the development of military courses of action.[23]

Dr. Brzezinski and his fellow planners comprised a so-called special coordination committee. The members included Defense Secretary Harold Brown; Admiral Stansfield Turner, director of the CIA; and probably at times, General David Jones; chairman of the Joint Chiefs of Staff; and Lieutenant General John S. Pustay, his assistant. This group convened secretly two or three times a week in Brzezinski's office (a clue that he was the first among equals) to plan the rescue. Brzezinski later acknowledged that he was "haunted" by the fear of exposure of the plan. His gravest concern, he wrote, was to ensure maximum secrecy and surprise, which he saw as a difficult task in view of the "pattern of massive leakage" of secrets within the government and the "endless multiplication of papers." The White House priority on maintaining secrecy characterized the operation from the start. Clearly, secrecy is vital to a covert raid but, as will be shown later in this account, excessive security fatally flawed the mission.[24]

Brzezinski was a leading advocate of a military rescue. A daring rescue at Tehran would put the Soviets and the world on notice that the United States could strike hard and quickly almost anywhere in the world. Brzezinski argued that a rescue would free the hostages and safeguard national honor. The successful raid would be seen as a stunning example of presidential courage. Because of the national security advisor's leading part in this plan, a brief background sketch is in order.

Brzezinski was born in Poland in 1928. As a child, he had accompanied his parents to Canada, where his father had been posted as consul general. After earning degrees at McGill University in Montreal, he received his doctorate in government in 1953 at Harvard. Subsequently he taught there and at Columbia University, where he served as director of the Research Institute on Communist Affairs. He became a U.S. citizen in 1958. As an expert in international relations, he came to the attention of David Rockefeller, president of the Chase-Manhattan Bank, who had a hand in selecting him as executive director of the prestigious Trilateral Commission, whose membership included America's corporate elite.* In this capacity he was called upon to brief his fellow Trilateralist, candidate Carter, on international topics during the race for the presidency. After the election, Brzezinski became the logical choice for national security advisor.[25]

Brzezinski's effervescent personality and his readiness to furnish reporters with pithy statements quickly made an impression on Washington, home of bureaucrats who normally shun colorful behavior and value discretion and prudence. He had no military experience, yet he became Carter's chief liaison with the Pentagon for what proved to be a very risky operation.

*Organized in 1973 by David Rockefeller, the Trilateral Commission's objective was to bring together national leaders of North America, Western Europe, and Japan to find solutions to global problems and to improve the world economy.

Dr. Zbigniew Brzezinski, President Carter's National Security Advisor and head of the Special Coordinating Committee for the rescue operation. (Defense Department)

As head of the committee, Brzezinski had no official command authority. As if to give substance to this fact, some days after the raid, Defense Secretary Brown took pains to make clear that in all matters relating to the operation the military reported to the defense secretary, who reported to the president. On the other hand, as the spokesman for the president, the energetic Brzezinski wielded a power that the Pentagon must have understood. Early on, he had visited the Pentagon and, according to Beckwith, "had instilled in the planners a feeling of urgency."[26]

It is a time-tested precept that a government should never mount a military operation unless it is prepared to use the force necessary to accomplish the objective. As did John F. Kennedy in the Bay of Pigs fiasco, Jimmy Carter authorized a high-risk, covert operation and then imposed excessive restrictions.[27] First, the White House instructed that an assault force be set to go immediately and that it be kept lean and small. Next, it decreed that maximum operational security (OPSEC) be enforced to ensure total surprise.

The Carter White House underestimated the armed forces' collective ability to maintain secrecy in large or small operations. Normandy in World War II and the Sontay raid in Vietnam are examples of military operations which maintained security. The services generally assume that a mission will succeed only if all hands are fully acquainted, on a need-to-know basis, with the roles of their fellow units and with the overall objective. Only then can individuals use their initiative and make effective decisions if things go wrong. These conditions did not prevail in the rescue operation.

Early in the planning, Brzezinski went on record as favoring a "generalized military response" in order to force Khomeini to release the prisoners. Specifically, he proposed that U.S. forces capture an Iranian port, clamp a naval blockade on the Persian Gulf, and send air strikes against Iran (presumably by carrier planes). After the Soviets invaded Afghanistan during Christmas week of 1979, he dismissed these ideas as counterproductive as they would have provided Moscow with justification for coming to the aid of a beleaguered Iran.[28]

But Brzezinski did not wholly abandon the idea of a broader military assault in conjunction with the rescue. Thus, when he suggested that the rescue be coordinated with an air strike (presumably by carrier planes), he reasoned that if the rescue mission failed, then President Carter could announce that he had authorized a successful punitive attack in retaliation for Iran's refusal to surrender the hostages. On the other hand, if the rescue mission succeeded, the strike "would be all to the good." As Brzezinski tells it, this scenario generated intense debate in the White House. As we shall see, on the day before the rescue mission was to be launched Carter canceled the strike. Meanwhile, the Joint Chiefs of Staff, having received the order to plan the rescue, began examining ways to execute it.

2

Planning the Assault

General Vaught, Task Force Commander

Shortly after the Pentagon learned of President Carter's intention to rescue the hostages, General Edward Meyer, army chief of staff, nominated Major General James B. Vaught, USA, to lead the task force. Even before the Iranians had seized the embassy in November 1979, Vaught had been selected to head an Army counterterrorist command, trained for clandestine missions abroad. At fifty-three, Vaught had a reputation as a top-flight officer in Ranger operations. Some observers saw him as the very model of a blood-and-guts soldier, cast in the John Wayne mold. Tall, broad-shouldered, outgoing, cheerful, and direct, he spoke with the accent of his native South.

Vaught attended The Citadel, the venerable military college in Charleston, South Carolina, for two years and then enlisted in the army in 1945. He was commissioned an infantry second lieutenant in 1947 at the age of twenty and qualified as a paratrooper. His service included duty in Germany, Japan, Korea, and Turkey. Among his combat decorations were two Silver Stars, two Bronze Stars, the Distinguished Flying

Cross, and the Purple Heart. He also was well acquainted with the Pentagon, having had tours in the Office of the Secretary of Defense, the Joint Staff, and at Army Headquarters. A graduate of the National War College in Washington, he had also earned a master's degree in international relations from George Washington University. After an outstanding record in Vietnam, Vaught was posted to the 18th Airborne Corps, Fort Bragg, North Carolina, where he was respected as a superb commander. One officer recalled that the day Vaught was promoted to brigadier general, the whole brigade rejoiced, so great was its regard for him.[1]

By late 1979 when General Meyer picked him for antiterrorist operations, Vaught, by now a major general, was known throughout the army for his exceptional ability to lead men in combat. Yet Vaught's experience as a battle-oriented officer did not prove sufficient for the planning of a complicated operation involving four services as well as sensitive dealings with the White House, all within five months. In hindsight, we can say that none of the planners fully grasped the long-range implications of President Carter's firm decrees—that, to protect the lives of the hostages, absolute secrecy be observed, that few individuals know of the plan, and that the size of the assault force be minimal.

The Penalty of Compartmentation

On 12 November 1979, General Vaught received orders to lead the rescue operation, the planning phase of which was named Rice Bowl (the operational phase was named Eagle Claw). A week earlier, the Joint Chiefs had set up a small, ad hoc group to develop ideas and organize a team to snatch the hostages in a lightning-quick raid. Three army officers, experts in unconventional combat tactics, were ordered from Fort Bragg, North Carolina, to strengthen the Pentagon's group. One was retired Major Richard J. Meadows, who later became an important secret agent in Tehran.[2] When General Vaught's staff was named, this ad hoc group ceased functioning.

After examining various schemes for rescuing the hostages, Vaught and General Jones agreed that a helicopter rescue had the greatest chance of success. Their plan called for a 40-hour-long operation using a combination of C-130 Hercules transports, helicopters, and commercial motor vehicles to gain entry into Tehran. In the first phase, six long-range Hercules aircraft would take off from a secret base in Egypt and transport to Desert One the assault force composed of Green Berets, a group of Army Rangers who would secure the landing zone, and huge rubber bladders filled with aviation fuel.★ Eight helicopters would fly from the aircraft carrier *Nimitz* in the Arabian Sea to Desert One. After refueling, the helicopters would then fly the Green Berets to Desert Two preparatory to a night rescue at the embassy compound.[3]

According to one account, the six C-130s destined for Desert One were scheduled as follows: three were to fly the assault force, the Ranger team, and the equipment, including camouflage netting for the helicopters at Desert Two; the other three aircraft would deliver eighteen thousand gallons of JP4 fuel. After the Rangers had secured the strip, two planes were to depart, leaving four Hercules to await the arrival of the helicopters. During the rescue at the embassy, two more C-130 gunships were to circle over the city, ready to fire on Iranian mobs or to destroy any Iranian fighter aircraft taking off from the local airport. General Vaught would direct this complex mission from his distant command post at Qena, Egypt. Satellite communications would link Vaught with his unit commanders, as well as with the Pentagon and the naval force in the Indian Ocean.[4] Counting the crews of the *Nimitz* battle group, thousands of American combat personnel and Iranian agents were involved in the operation that was to have enabled Beckwith's men to spirit the hostages out of Tehran.

General Vaught was responsible for preserving security by ensuring that no one group was aware of operational details

★A Ranger is a U.S. soldier trained in raiding tactics. A Green Beret is a U.S. soldier who is a member of the Army Special Forces trained to develop allied guerrillas and seek out and kill enemy guerrillas.

of another unit unless there was an absolute need to know. This procedure is known as compartmentation. How was it possible to expect Vaught and his staff to select qualified men, train them in special assault techniques, and, finally, blend elements of time, distance, people, and equipment into an exacting schedule of events—all under the constraints of compartmentation? Although Vaught was authorized to shape the rescue plan as he saw fit, he was also expected to accede to the Joint Chiefs' directives on matters such as task force organization and security. Thus, when they set down their requirement for compartmentation, Vaught was expected to carry out their orders.

For reasons of security the JCS consciously chose not to implement their Contingency Plan (CONPLAN) on the grounds that too many people might be involved and secrecy jeopardized. For the same reason they decided not to use a current JCS-developed framework for a Joint Task Force (JTF). As a result, when General Vaught assumed command on 12 November, he found that he was not authorized to use the existing JTF structure, upon which he could have quickly built his special force, but instead was forced to resort to ad hoc methods.

It was the opinion of the Holloway investigators that, because of security considerations, many things that could have been done to improve mission success were not done. The reason, said the investigators, stemmed from the lack of a more precise security plan for the task force. Until all the evidence becomes available, we shall not know if General Vaught's security plan was imposed on him by the JCS or whether he originated the plan himself and obtained JCS concurrence.

Although maintaining secrecy was paramount, the security measures put into place to do that should have been more carefully tailored to the task force's operational requirements. During the actual operation, overemphasis on or misapplication of security measures seriously hampered communication between task force units, particularly in regard to emergencies.[5]

Brzezinski later described his fear that leaks within those official circles concerned with planning would compromise the rescue. His concern that "the mission would be destroyed" by lack of security helps to explain why the Joint Chiefs and Vaught held in abeyance their organized and well-oiled CONPLAN and JTF organization plan, relying more on improvised arrangements for the rescue plan.[6]

It is important to note that even if the task force had used a more effective security plan, the rescue might not have succeeded. We shall address later the question of whether Vaught's force (assuming it was functioning at top efficiency) was suitable for the task at hand.

Despite constraints, Vaught may well have been subjected to White House pressure to expedite his plans. As the Holloway report tells it, "a sense of urgency was impressed on COMJTF [Commander Joint Task Force, General Vaught] and his staff at the very outset: that an immediate operation was required." Left unsaid was that the armed forces were not prepared to field this special task force on short notice. Moreover, the smooth rhythm of training was disrupted by sudden White House alerts that the rescue force be ready. According to one officer, the Green Berets received seven such warnings before the actual D-day of 24 April 1980.[7]

If and when General Jones and General Vaught publish their memoirs, they may shed light on the amount of "guidance" (a Pentagon euphemism for "do it this way") issued by the White House. The Holloway panel was not in a position to comment on this aspect, but Dr. Brzezinski's *New York Times Magazine* article depicts an ever-active national security advisor consulting with Defense Secretary Brown and urging the president to expand the operation. It is likely that the bustling Brzezinski actively influenced the mission planning.

A Flawed Chain of Command

A peculiar feature of Vaught's task force was the status of an officer who outranked him. Major General Philip G. Gast, USAF, was assistant for readiness, Tactical Air Command, when he was appointed "special consultant" for the task force.

General David C. Jones, USAF, chairman of
the Joint Chiefs of Staff at the time of the
aborted rescue. According to Admiral Holloway, the Joint Chiefs believed that the operation had a 60 to 70 percent chance of success.
(U.S. Air Force)

On 1 April 1980, he was promoted to the rank of lieutenant
general. Because of special experience gained during a recent
tour in Tehran as head of the U.S. military mission, Gast had
first-hand knowledge of the city, and, as Colonel Beckwith
noted, he could identify U.S. personnel, formerly in Iran,

Major General James B. Vaught posed for
this photo in the Pentagon a short time before
the luckless rescue attempt. He later became a
lieutenant general. (U.S. Army)

who could answer questions. Unfortunately, his senior rank
generated confusion in the chain of command, which affected
the training of the helicopter force.[8]

Early in the planning, Colonel Charles H. Pitman,
USMC, an assistant to General Jones, was ordered to become
involved in the planning and execution of the helicopter phase.
Surprisingly, in view of these orders, Pitman was not offi-

Lieutenant General Philip C. Gast, USAF, was brought into the operation because of his special knowledge of Tehran, where he had served previously. Under an informal arrangement, he also supervised the training program for the helicopter crews, a responsibility he presumably shared with Marine Colonel Charles Pitman. The Holloway review group was critical of this clouded chain of command. (U.S. Air Force)

cially designated a member of the task force staff. Neverthe-less, he examined plans, checked the helicopter aircrew selec-tions for special mission qualifications, arranged for more seasoned pilots, evaluated progress in training, and was re-sponsible for the transfer of personnel to the Marine Corps Air Station at Yuma, Arizona, a base close to the desert training areas. He requested and was granted permission to attend General Vaught's planning meetings. By the middle of Janu-ary 1980, Pitman had assumed a de facto status of leadership simply because no one else had been officially assigned. In this informal role, Pitman's responsibility for helicopter training inevitably conflicted with that of General Gast, who was concerned with the training of the pilots. Gast was qualified in jets but not helicopters.

Pitman's status was further clouded by the naming of Lieutenant Colonel Edward R. Seiffert, USMC, as helicopter flight leader. Presumably, he was subordinate to Colonel Pit-man, who was de facto deputy task force commander (heli-copters). Yet General Vaught apparently never formally spelled out the command chain from himself and General Gast to Colonel Pitman and Lieutenant Colonel Seiffert. At issue is the question of who was responsible for the unit's attaining "special mission" capability. This was no small task: within four months the unit was supposed to master the technique of flying six hundred nautical miles at night over deserts and mountains to a desert rendezvous; to become proficient in refueling from the C-130s at the site; to fly on to a mountain hideout; and finally to perfect techniques in landing at night in a soccer stadium or within the embassy compound. No heli-copter unit had ever trained for a similar task.

Indeed, in view of the demands placed upon the helicop-ters and the length of time in hostile territory, such an opera-tion had never before been attempted. There was only a lim-ited amount of useful information that could be drawn from the raids at Entebbe and Mogadishu, as they were so unlike the Iranian rescue plan. These rescues were relatively simple; no helicopters were involved and the time in enemy territory was short. In the absence of any precedent, how was the decision reached to go ahead?

The White House desperately wanted the rescue, even though the risks were high, and the Joint Chiefs approved the plan as being consistent with "national policy objectives." Yet, the Holloway investigators found that, because of the plan's complexity, any estimate of the overall probability for success could only be conjecture and that it was virtually impossible to appraise the chances of success of the phase of the rescue from Desert One on to Tehran. It was, the investigators concluded, a high-risk operation with little margin for mistakes or bad luck. We must assume that the president and his advisors, both civilian and military, while acknowledging that the risk was great, decided that the goal was worth the gamble. Only later did the high-level errors in decision making and planning come to light and result in a major shakeup of the nations's Special Operations Forces (SOF).

One of these failures in decision making lay in Vaught's choosing not to formally designate an overall helicopter force leader. Some critics assert that the lack of a clear command chain, wherein each officer had defined responsibilities and authority, seriously hampered the uncovering of weaknesses that surfaced later during the operation. Military officers, and business leaders as well, know that if an individual reports to two or more persons, it is likely that everyone's understanding of procedures and policy will be confused. With Pitman reporting to both Gast and Vaught, this case was no exception.

According to the Holloway investigators, it was not clear during training whether Pitman commanded the helicopter unit. "It was implied that this officer [Pitman] was in charge of the helicopter force during the preparation phase, and he believed this to be so," but during November and December 1979, General Vaught thought that General Gast was directing much (if not all) of the training. Gast did in fact, in addition to his role as consultant on Iran, try to lift some of the training burden from Vaught's shoulders. Gast was a frequent visitor at training sites in the western Nevada desert where he observed and reported on the helicopters and C-130 air training.[9]

On 12 April 1980, only twelve days before the actual operation, Gast was named deputy task force commander. The reason for the delay in designating him has yet to be explained but, no doubt, was part of the operational security plan to prevent leaks or even to avoid publicizing the anomaly of a lieutenant general serving under an officer junior to him.

Despite speculation in the media that the helicopter chain of command, during the operation, was uncertain, strong evidence exists that Colonel Pitman, probably also on 12 April was named deputy commander for helicopters under General Vaught. In fact, the Holloway Report indirectly identifies Pitman on page 51, when it uses the term, the "Deputy Commander for Helicopters" [Pitman]. The same paragraph also refers to the "helicopter flight commander" [Seiffert].★

To lead the assault on the embassy, Vaught chose Colonel Charlie A. Beckwith. Known in military circles as "Chargin' Charlie," Beckwith, fifty-one years of age, had grown up in Atlanta. After several years as an ROTC student at the University of Georgia, where he had played on the football team, he joined the army. A veteran of the Korean Conflict, he fought for three years as a Green Beret in Indochina, where he sustained a near-fatal chest wound. Plainspoken and hard-bitten, Beckwith was best known for his specialty of unconventional warfare. One journalist wrote

---

★Colonel J. L. McManaway, USMC, a senior Marine pilot and, in 1984, director of public affairs at Marine Corps Headquarters, has informed this writer that he learned from Seiffert that Colonel Pitman did, indeed, during the actual operation, hold the post of deputy commander for helicopters. Colonel McManaway revealed that Lieutenant Colonel Seiffert was one of his squadron officers in Vietnam and was a "superb pilot and leader." According to McManaway, Lieutenant Colonel Seiffert affirmed that, during the mission, Colonel Pitman was his immediate superior and that Pitman reported to the task force commander. The above should put to rest any doubts that during the actual operation the helicopter chain of command was blurred.

that on his desk was a sign reading "Kill 'em all. Let God sort 'em out." At the time of his appointment to the Tehran team, he was stationed at Fort Bragg as the commander of a crack unit of Green Berets known as the Delta Force, which had been set up in 1977 to train for antiterrorist operations."[10]

To command the Air Force component, General Vaught named Colonel James Kyle, USAF. His primary responsibility was that of directing and coordinating the C-130 training. Kyle had been selected in part because of his experience in Air Force special (commando) operations. Fortunately, neither Colonel Kyle nor Colonel Beckwith was plagued with the command problem faced by Colonel Pitman.[11]

Pitfalls for the Joint Chiefs

In its examination of the ill-fated mission, the Holloway panel probed the question, To what extent were General Vaught's vexing planning problems understood by the Joint Chiefs? In the all-too-frenetic atmosphere of the Pentagon, the Chiefs may have relied too much on Vaught's staff briefings to assure themselves that planning for the raid was progressing satisfactorily. After all, General Vaught wore two stars; his record in combat was unmatched; and he had been recommended for command of the task force by the army chief of staff himself.

The Holloway panel addressed in low-key terms the disturbing fact that the Chiefs received only a few briefings on the plan. The panel noted that on the three occasions when the Chiefs were briefed on the status and content of the operation, no independent experts were there to speak on the plan. Their acquiescence to only three briefings suggests that the Chiefs may not have fully comprehended the plan's complexities, the potential pitfalls, and the vital necessity to subject the plan to merciless examination. Why did the Chiefs not seek out more information on such factors as, for example, weather forecasts and helicopter reliability? Why did they not press for the use of C-130 pathfinder planes to guide the helicopters and to warn them of any navigational difficulties ahead?[12]

The Chiefs were dealing with a special warfare, unconventional operation, but their backgrounds had not qualified them as special warfare experts. General Jones had held important air commands in Vietnam and Europe. Admiral Thomas B. Hayward, a former fleet commander, was an expert in naval warfare. General Meyer was a proven army commander, while Marine General Robert H. Barrow was a specialist in amphibious warfare. None of them had firsthand experience in special operations, and evidence suggests that the JCS overview of the mission plan was, at best, limited. Why, then, had the Joint Chiefs denied themselves the benefit of an objective evaluation, an advantage they routinely enjoyed when considering less sensitive operations?

At the outset of the planning, the JCS had considered establishing a small group of carefully selected individuals with strong backgrounds in special operations. They would review the rescue plan as it developed and provide the Chiefs with their views. This idea of a panel of experts was abandoned, as the Holloway investigators revealed, because of an overriding fear of breaching security. The investigators did not identify who made the "conscious decision not to form such an element," but the aim was clearly to limit the number of people privy to the plan. Whether the decision came from the White House or not the effect was the same: the Joint Chiefs and Vaught's task force planners analyzed their own plan for feasibility and suitability, with all the inherent dangers of such self-criticism.

One may well ask why did the Chiefs not protest to their civilian superiors this lack of devil's advocates to conduct a minute review. We do not know whether they did object or whether they were overruled. We do learn from the Holloway report that General Vaught was fully aware of the disadvantages arising from the lack of a murder board. Consequently, he directed his officers to check each component of the plan for soundness, through rigorous drills simulating the various phases of the mission. In hindsight, it is clear that this method was not enough to uncover certain operational weaknesses that doomed the rescue.

The Chiefs of Staff who approved the rescue plan. Admiral Thomas Hayward, chief of naval operations, later said in a speech that if the Chiefs led the president down the wrong path by recommending the mission, then the blame resided with them. Left to right: General Edward C. Meyer, USA; Admiral Thomas B. Hayward, USN; General David C. Jones, USAF, chairman; General Lew Allen, Jr., USAF; General Robert H. Barrow, USMC. (Defense Department)

The Joint Chiefs came under mild criticism from the Holloway group for failing to set up a "useful testing mechanism" (murder board). Such a separate plans-review board would have been invaluable to the Chiefs, as proposals would have been evaluated by disinterested experts.

Admittedly, the tight security surrounding the mission was successful in that there were no leaks. Whether more selective and flexible security procedures would have strengthened the task force's effectiveness while maintaining secrecy remains a controversial issue. But on balance, later mishaps and bungles during the actual operation were traceable to the excessive compartmentation imposed on General Vaught.

A Waste of Intelligence Resources

A competent intelligence staff is indispensable in planning any covert operation, a rule General Vaught fully understood. Why then did he not arrange to use the fully staffed and integrated intelligence component already in operation under the aegis of the JCS? Instead, the general named his own J-2 (joint task force intelligence officer) and gave him a small staff. The arrangement proved insufficient for the job at hand.

The Holloway panel noted this deficiency and, avoiding direct criticism, stated that "a preferred approach [to forming an intelligence staff] would have been to task the Director, DIA [Defense Intelligence Agency] to establish a small and highly select interagency Intelligence Task Force (ITF) in direct support of the JTF [Joint Task Force]. . . ." The director of the DIA is, in effect, the intelligence officer for the JCS. The ITF could have organized selected units of the entire U.S. intelligence community in short order. Vaught's own J-2 (intelligence officer) could have enjoyed constant access to the ITF. Division of responsibility on intelligence collection could have been avoided because the DIA director would also have been the head of the ITF with direct access to all other agency directors. Under such an arrangement, Vaught, spared the heavy burden of intelligence management, which must have absorbed much of his attention, would have been able to invest more time supervising the all-important training program.

As it developed, however, Vaught's J-2 acquired liaison officers from, probably, the CIA, the DIA, the National Security Agency, and the State Department's Bureau of Intelligence and Research. These officers were to serve as conduits for information between the task force and their parent agencies. But the system proved sluggish. The intelligence officer and his three assistants had to prod into action a mass of faceless individuals in several agencies spread all over the Washington area. Administrative drag is a common hazard in government. Had the DIA director, a three-star general, been in charge, however, we may assume that the collection of intelligence would have been vastly speeded up.[13]

Compartmentation imposed by security was also a barrier to the transmission of intelligence. Delays occurred because most intelligence officers outside the J-2 staff were not briefed on the complete mission, although certain individuals who worked on operational requirements were able to divine the rough outlines of the plan. These officers believed, as the Holloway panel discovered, that they could have rendered more effective support if they had been advised at the outset. Compartmentation bore a bitter harvest. Weather officers, for one instance, were aware of the possibility of dust clouds over the Iranian desert but were not authorized to talk directly to the helicopter pilots. In another instance, Vaught's meteorologists prepared a weather annex describing dust clouds, but, as the Holloway investigators discovered, the helicopter pilots never saw this document.[14]

Problems in Intelligence Collection

General Vaught faced a number of difficult intelligence tasks, among which were the following:
- Find a remote desert site where the helicopters could refuel from air-dropped fuel bladders. When this proved infeasi-

ble, find a remote landing strip suitable for receiving six C-130 transport planes and eight helicopters
- Insert secret agents into Tehran and arrange for their communication with Washington
- Locate a hiding place within about two hours driving time from Tehran to shield the rescue force during fourteen hours of daylight
- Locate a suitable airfield in a friendly nation within flight distance of Iran both to serve as a launching point and, possibly, to receive the C-130s after the mission
- Locate an airstrip in a friendly nation near the Arabian Sea for refueling the C-130s
- Find out exactly, by agent reports and satellite photography, where the hostages were being held within the 27-acre embassy compound
- Transfer eight helicopters from the United States to an aircraft carrier in the Indian Ocean without arousing suspicion.

All of these matters required collection, analysis, and collation of data and photo interpretation. The entire endeavor needed first-class intelligence support.

In addition to the lack of an efficient processing system, the intelligence effort was hampered because many experienced "old hands" had been retired from the CIA. Consequently, when the Iranian mob took over the U.S. Embassy on 4 November 1979, the CIA had not one agent operating in Tehran. Why had the agency cut back on covert intelligence collection? The answer may well be that the administration believed that it could safely disband the "dirty tricks" units dealing with covert operations because the CIA could rely more on high-technology devices such as satellite photography and sophisticated electronic monitoring equipment rather than on human agents. In any event, General Vaught initially lacked adequate intelligence.

Vaught's J-2, however, soon provided Beckwith with photos of the embassy compound plus information on the six buildings where the hostages probably were held. Satellite photography contributed to the effort. Other intelligence was gleaned from television news programs showing the Iranian guards, the streets, and the nine-foot wall surrounding the embassy. The data were useful in constructing a large-scale model of the compound.

As the planning progressed, problems arose in the transmission of information. Unwittingly, the J-2 staff sometimes failed to distribute incoming intelligence to officers who had a valid interest in the information. For example, an intelligence analyst, who might be working on a specific subject, would learn by chance of a pertinent report some days after it had been circulated to Vaught's planners. Moreover, because of the need for immediate intelligence, Vaught's J-2 staff officers sometimes sent raw or only partially evaluated reports to officers preparing the operation plan. This less-than-desirable dissemination probably would not have occurred if the DIA director had been in charge. In citing these deficiencies, the Holloway panel stated that the intelligence support was "adequate," not exactly glowing praise. The panel recommended that in future covert operations where time was critical, the Joint Chiefs should from the beginning place the DIA director in charge of an interagency intelligence unit to support the task force.[15]

The most sensitive and dangerous element in intelligence collection was that of placing agents inside Tehran. Two years after the operation, journalist David C. Martin of *Newsweek* published a sensational cover story revealing how it was done. Martin focused on the exploits of a retired Green Beret, Major Richard J. Meadows, who, masquerading as an Irish businessman, walked the streets of Tehran unchallenged. This intrepid agent helped to arrange for the rental of a warehouse and the purchase of vehicles needed for the secret transfer of Beckwith's Green Berets from Desert Two to Tehran. Meadows's hazardous work came to naught when President Carter gave the order to abort the mission. Fortunately, all U.S. agents, including two army men and an air force sergeant, were quickly notified by radio and made their way to safety.

Jimmy Carter writes that U.S. agents (among whom was an anti-Khomeini Iranian) moved freely in the city and reported on the security routine of the Iranian guards. They were unable, however, to gain specific information on the location of the prisoners within the compound. This intelligence providentially fell into the hands of a U.S. agent only hours before the operation was to get under way.

Reportedly, three days before the rescue operation began, a Pakistani cook at the American embassy was allowed by the Iranian government to leave the country. After boarding a plane for Ankara, Turkey, he sat down beside a man who was a deep-cover U.S. agent. We have no means of judging whether he was there by design or by sheer chance. But the agent and his colleagues in Ankara did obtain from the cook the locations of the hostages in the chancellery (the administration building) and of the various Iranian guards.

Colonel Beckwith received this last-minute, and priceless, intelligence at Qena, Egypt, on 23 April 1980 and quickly modified his assault plan by eliminating a dangerous, time-consuming search of four buildings where the hostages might have been held, concentrating instead on the chancellery.[16] The fact that the White House had approved the original plan suggests that the Carter administration was prepared to "do something," even without all the information it should have had.

Setting the Size of the Force

A major question facing Vaught's planners was that of fixing the size of the task force. As the Holloway report makes clear, each time Vaught received intelligence that caused him to order a change in the number of men, a domino effect generated changes in equipment and in the number of aircraft. Vaught originally had estimated a task force of about 80 men. By D-day this figure had grown to well over 250, of which 132 were to be airlifted to Desert One.

In their postraid analysis, the investigators expressed sympathy for Vaught in his difficult choice of setting the number of men, noting that a commander is always tempted to make any adjustments possible to improve his posture up to the point when the battle is joined. The Holloway group went on to counsel that in any future planning of a special mission, "such late changes be made with some trepidation and extraordinary care." It softened its criticism by observing that it would have been desirable for Vaught to have fixed the "airlift requirement" (the number of men and the quantity of their equipment) well in advance of D-day and to hold to that ceiling unless a "compelling case" would have warranted an increase. By not setting the troop-lift ceiling in early January, Vaught unknowingly generated perturbations that affected the entire preparation period.[17]

As the task force increased in size, the training, logistics, and personnel requirements expanded proportionally. If the JCS had opted for their own Contingency Plan with its built-in structures for organization, training, and development, then the instabilities in personnel selection and training (described later in this account) would undoubtedly have been substantially reduced. If General Vaught had used the Con-Plan, the panel stated, he would have had "the trusted agents, the built-in OPSEC [operational security], the secure communications. At a minimum, COMJTF [General Vaught, the commander, joint task force] would have had a running start and could have devoted more hours to plans, operations, and tactics, rather than to administration and logistics."

Choosing the Right Helicopter

The selection of the right type of helicopter raised a series of provocative issues for the task force staff. The helo so chosen had to be capable of taking off from a carrier, flying six hundred miles at altitudes as low as five hundred feet over desert and as high as eleven thousand feet over mountains. Its heavy payload would have to include state-of-the-art radios and electronic navigational equipment for instrument flying. For the flight from Desert One to Desert Two, the aircraft would carry Beckwith's men, most of them laden with heavy packs, weapons, and explosives.

The necessity for the helos to take off from a carrier

raised other considerations. The HH-53, which was specifically equipped for special operations, was just coming off the production line and had yet to demonstrate its reliability. Vaught's staff learned that the HH-53 could not fit onto a carrier elevator (a lift to carry aircraft between the flight deck and the hangar deck below) without a time-consuming removal of its rotor blades. Furthermore, few pilots had qualified in its new systems, and it carried less payload than the Navy's RH-53D. Thus, the HH-53 was ruled out.[18]

The staff also examined the characteristics of other models: the CH-46, CH-47, CH-53, and RH-53. While each would fit into an Air Force C-5 transport plane, for airlift to a base in the Indian Ocean area, none had the desired combination of range, payload, automatic pilot, and shipboard compatibility. The RH-53D, however, did. Better yet, it was easily provided with spare parts from the navy's supply system. If the RH-53D were carrier-based before the operation began, then obviously the maintenance crews would avoid any administrative misunderstanding that might arise if army or air force helicopters were used. Yet another reason prompted the choice. Because aircraft carriers in the Indian Ocean were under Soviet surveillance by trailing ships, aircraft, and satellites, the navy's RH-53D was the only type of possible helo for the mission that would not arouse Russian suspicion. So the decision settled on the Sea Stallion.

The Sea Stallion was built by the Sikorsky division of United Technologies at Stratford, Connecticut. It could carry between thirty and fifty people, depending on the fuel load, at speeds up to 196 miles per hour. The eight helicopters assigned for the mission were built between June 1973 and December 1975 and had proved reliable and rugged as aerial minesweepers. In this role, the aircraft, presumably, would not excite interest among Soviet intelligence experts if they were spotted on board the *Nimitz*.*

---

*The RH-53D was primarily employed to detonate acoustic and magnetic influence mines. The helicopters towed a sled fitted with a generator which emitted electric energy through a trailing electrode or a noise device. These energy pulses were designed to detonate any acoustic or

How Many Helicopters Were Enough?

Much of the criticism that erupted after the disaster at Desert One was aimed at the alleged lack of helicopters to carry out the mission. In analyzing this charge, one must bear in mind the White House desire that the rescue force be kept small. Thus, early rescue plans considered by Vaught's staff called for only four helicopters. As his officers gathered more intelligence and studied the problem, they increased the number of men in the attack group, forcing a corresponding increase in helicopters, whose number grew from four, to six, to seven, and finally to eight. Meteorological conditions also influenced the number of helicopters: The warmer the temperatures, the less weight helicopters can carry, and thus the seasonal temperature rise anticipated in Iran would cause a proportionate loss of helicopter lift capability.[19]

Colonel Pitman, as quoted by Beckwith, pointed out in early January 1980, that if a commander needs two helicopters, then, because of their undependability, he actually needs three. He suggested to Beckwith that they should recommend to General Vaught that without six functioning helicopters at Desert One, the mission should not go forward. The two officers then approached Vaught, who agreed that they should have a minimum of six ready at Desert One. Implied was the understanding that nine aircraft would be put on board the *Nimitz*. As he recounts in his book, however, Beckwith was told later that only eight RH-53Ds could fit on the hangar deck of the *Nimitz*. In November 1983, he revealed in a radio interview that sometime "later" he was told (he did not name

influence mine within range. Although the sled could be rigged to sweep for mechanical mines by means of cable cutters, by the 1980s this type of mine was obsolescent. The navy had only twenty-four RH-53Ds, and by transferring eight to General Vaught, the navy drew down its minesweeping capacity by one-third. The transfer also meant that a proportionate number of naval technicians had to be assigned to maintain these helicopters. Interestingly enough, in the mid-1970s, the Shah of Iran purchased six Sea Stallions for his navy.

his source) that eleven helicopters could have been positioned on the hangar deck.

As the investigators learned, General Vaught's planners conducted a risk-analysis based on RH-53D statistical data. Their findings "seemed to support" the planners' conclusion that eight helos "provided an acceptable degree of risk." Moreover, the need for secrecy, as perceived by the Carter administration, was a strong reason for deciding on the minimum number that, in their judgment, could carry out the mission.[20]

According to the Holloway panel, "an unconstrained planner would have more than likely required at least 10 helicopters, 11 under the most likely case, and up to 12 using peacetime historical data."[21] More helicopters were available, and their use could have reduced the risk of termination. Additionally, the Holloway panel stated that the carrier Nimitz could have accommodated a few more helicopters with no penalty to its other flight missions, that is, the Nimitz could have launched and recovered its attack aircraft and surveillance planes with even twelve RH-53Ds on board.

But would there have been sufficient fuel available for extra helicopters at Desert One to carry out the flights to Tehran and beyond? Again, the investigators answered in the affirmative for at least ten helicopters. Thus, there was every reason to believe—save the debatable issue of operational security—that eleven helicopters could have taken off from the Nimitz and that Colonel Beckwith's attack force conceivably could have departed Desert One in ten helicopters. For these reasons, the official investigating panel contended that more helicopters should have been used, although such an increase of itself would not have ensured success. The panel's finding coincided with the "rule of 100 percent" traditionally used in commando raids. Thus, if Beckwith needed six helicopters at the soccer stadium, then twelve RH-53Ds should have taken off from the Nimitz.[22]

Surprisingly, Brzezinski describes how at one of his meetings Lieutenant General John S. Pustay, an assistant to

General Jones, whispered to Brzezinski's deputy, David Aaron, that "we needed to take a closer look at the helicopter part of the operation." Why would a three-star general be reluctant to bring the matter of helicopter strength out in the open? Did Brzezinski or Carter previously announce that the limit would be seven helos? And why did not General Jones himself speak up, rather than his assistant?

After listening to Aaron, and taking a "closer" look, Brzezinski recalled, "We decided to increase the number to eight." He justified the increase as providing more redundance without the need to expand the number of C-130s. As Brzezinski tells it, he had been previously informed "by the military" (Vaught? Jones? the JCS?) that seven helicopters would provide a sufficient margin of safety. Why, with a short time to go, would the task force commander be in doubt as to how many helicopters were needed?

Brzezinski falls into error when he compares the Tehran mission with Entebbe. The latter was a swift, "fast-in, fast-out" operation where deception and concealment were minor problems. Its rescue tactics—the Israelis spent only ninety minutes on the ground—and the logistics were simple in contrast to General Vaught's complicated plan. The two operations were not comparable in magnitude.

Brzezinski subsequently defended the size of the force, arguing that if twice as many helicopters had been used Iran might have "discovered the mission because of the air armada penetrating their air space." He reasoned that the United States would then have been charged with "typically American redundancy" and with an unwillingness to use a small, effective force as the Israelis did at Entebbe.[23]

We can question whether the demands for secrecy and a "small" operation could have persuaded the Pentagon, initially, to accept a bare-bones force of seven helicopters until better military judgment prompted a last-minute request for eight. Two years after the raid, Colonel Beckwith reminded us that

> there were some very heavy people in Washington who
> were participating in this, and sometimes we would say

"How about this?" and they wouldn't know what in hell we were talking about.

He went on to say that occasionally he had to put his foot down and announce, "If these things do not occur, then me and my guys are not going to go." Beckwith regretted that he had not registered his objections more often.[24]

The Problem of Pilot Selection

In late November 1979 General Vaught was being pressed by the White House to mount the rescue whenever a "window of opportunity" opened. Accordingly, he initially selected navy and marine helicopter pilots experienced in carrier and assault operations. Six marine pilots received emergency orders on Thanksgiving Eve to report at once to the Marine base at Cherry Point, North Carolina. Other marine pilots came from West Coast bases. Probably the navy pilots were drawn from the helicopter minesweeping squadron that provided the RH-53Ds.

The planning staff's haste in recruiting helicopter pilots created an unexpected problem. General Vaught had originally planned to place marine aviators in the right-hand (pilot's) seat and navy pilots in the left hand (copilot's) seat. His reason was sound: the marine pilots were trained in flight techniques for special operations, while their navy counterparts were familiar with the operating characteristics of the Sea Stallion. But it shortly became obvious that some pilots were having trouble mastering special flight maneuvers such as tight-formation flying at night without landmarks.

When the first night rehearsal exposed serious pilot deficiencies, Vaught ordered a widespread search for twenty of the best pilots in the armed forces. More than two hundred aviators were screened, according to Admiral Holloway. The majority of those finally selected were marine officers, with two navy aviators and one air force officer. Lieutenant Colonel Edward R. Seiffert, USMC, was named as flight leader. In late December 1979, the newly chosen pilots, upon reporting to the USMC Air Station, Yuma, Arizona, were sent for training at the Army Proving Ground, also at Yuma. Unfortunately, several weeks of valuable training time had been lost.[25]

The Holloway group was surprised that Vaught did not order the personnel from an entire Marine CH-53 helicopter squadron to man the mission aircraft. A believable cover story could have been spread to explain the shift. If Vaught had chosen this course, then the result, in the opinion of the Holloway panel, would have been an integrated, trained unit with established procedures, which needed no shakedown period. If individual pilots and crewmen had to be replaced, transfers could have been accomplished fairly easily. Most important, the squadron would have benefited from a built-in unity in morale, tactics, and administration. All hands would have known each other and been familiar with the information channels in use.

Admitting the wisdom of hindsight, the Holloway group nevertheless proposed another option for the selection of pilots. The panel observed that "USAF pilots, more experienced in the mission profile envisioned for the rescue operation, would have probably progressed more rapidly" than navy and marine pilots who had not mastered the techniques required for a complex, secret mission over rugged terrain. Implied was whether Vaught should have asked himself if he actually needed navy and marine pilots simply because they were familiar with carrier operations and amphibious assaults. Or should he also have considered air force helicopter pilots qualified in special operations and in long-range flights at night over unfamiliar territory? Moreover, air force pilots (experienced in unconventional operations) could have easily adapted to a few, new, technical changes in the Navy RH-53D.[26]

The panel was correct in its assumption. In 1961 an air force special operations project known as "Jungle Jim" had demonstrated that a pilot could "transition" with relative ease to an aircraft of similar design and performance. But this same pilot would find it much harder to learn the novel, even unique, skills required for covert missions. That is to say, a pilot could learn to fly another helicopter model much more easily than he could acquire a new psychological attitude to cope with the dangers of special operations. Presumably, qualified air force pilots would already have acquired such a mind-set, while marine and navy aviators would be obliged to spend precious time doing so.

Such air force helicopter pilots were available from personnel records listing the names of 114 qualified H-53 pilots, instructors, and flight examiners. Of these air force officers, 96 were competent in long-range flight. Moreover, the air force roster carried the names of 86 former H-53 pilots, most of whom had had experience in special operations or combat rescue, probably in Vietnam, among other places. Most of these pilots would have been psychologically prepared for the pressures of secret missions; they would have probably progressed faster in training. So one could conclude, in theory at least, that ideally Vaught's team should have been made up of air force special operations pilots and marine aviators chosen for their skill in assault operations.

The Holloway report was quick to acknowledge that there was no evidence suggesting that any other combination of air crew would have performed better than those who flew on 24 April 1980. The report emphasized, however, that in future operations the military high command should designate an entire operational helicopter unit, trained in advance, to be ready whenever called for a special mission. General Vaught did not enjoy such an advantage in December 1979.

3

Countdown to D-day

The Heat of Public Opinion

Even as Vaught's combat team trained in North Carolina and in the western desert, Americans, tuned to the evening news, heard nightly the count of days the hostages had been held by the Iranians. American television screens offered daily spectacles of chanting Iranian mobs burning U.S. flags and mugging for the cameras. Khomeini's men quickly recognized that the foreign journalists in Tehran were a means to publicize Iran's grievances to a world audience, an unintended gift that could not have been bought for any sum. The humiliating scenes angered U.S. voters and eroded their confidence in Carter's ability to resolve the crisis. Politicians, with an eye to the coming elections, sensed the public clamor, and in February 1980 some forty members of Congress met with Brzezinski to voice their frustrations over the president's inability to budge Khomeini.

The *Wall Street Journal* proposed a military solution, calling on the administration to note that U.S. forces had the capability to rescue the hostages by employing elite paratroopers and huge helicopters that could fly hundreds of miles

undetected at night. Army Green Berets had already demonstrated their skill in special operations in Vietnam; a similar
raid into Tehran could not be ruled out, declared the *Journal*.
The similarity between this prescription and the proposed
rescue plan may have spurred Brzezinski in his efforts to
induce Carter to approve the raid.[1]

Other news journals reported that Carter was in a precar-
ious political position. *Time* pointed to the voting public's
anger and discontent and declared that Carter might have a far
more difficult time in beating the Republican candidate,
Ronald Reagan, than supposed early in the campaign. *U.S.
News & World Report* remarked on the sense of hopelessness
evident in the White House over the hostage issue.

The administration's customary reliance on moderation
and reasonableness was proving well-nigh futile in dealing
with the Ayatollah. In the United States, disgust with Iran's
refusal to negotiate was mingled with indignation over the
protracted stalemate. Thus, the feeling in the White House
that it was reaching the end of the diplomatic line coupled with
the public's demand for results seemed sufficient reason for
taking direct action. It remains for future historians to decide
to what extent Carter's approval of the raid derived from his
humanitarian concern for the hostages' safety and to what
extent it sprang from his need, in an election year, to "do
something."[2]

Choosing a Landing Site

During the first six weeks of the planning, Vaught had
counted on the helicopters to refuel in the desert from fuel
blivets (large flexible bladders) dropped by parachute by C-
130s at night. After numerous rehearsals had demonstrated
that the blivets might be dropped in inaccessible spots, the idea
was abandoned. Instead, the C-130 tankers would land on the
desert floor and refuel the helicopters alongside. Once this
decision was made, General Vaught's staff called on the intelligence agencies to locate a landing strip in Iran remote from
Tehran and suitable as a rendezvous for the six C-130s and the

COUNTDOWN TO D-DAY   47

eight helicopters. The search was not an easy one. Iran, a country of 636,000 square miles, is essentially a vast plateau surrounded by mountains. Helicopters, launched from a ship in the Arabian Sea, would have to fly over two ranges of the rugged Zagros Mountains, rising to an average height of 4,000 feet with occasional peaks of 11,000 feet. Once clear of the ranges, the aircraft would fly over desert terrain to the rendezvous, identified, most probably, with the aid of satellite photography. The possible site lay 265 nautical miles southeast of Tehran in a giant salt desert known as Dasht-e-Kavir. There remained the task of checking the firmness of the soil to accommodate the landings of the heavy (some 80 tons) C-130s.

Brzezinski writes that on 28 February 1980 he broached to the president the idea of sending a reconnaissance plane into Iran to scout a possible landing site. The president rejected the notion, concerned that he might jeopardize negotiations with Khomeini, should the probe fail and the plane be shot down. Brzezinski, on 7 March 1980, raised the issue again, and met with the same reaction. Meanwhile, time was running out because the hours of darkness in Iran were growing shorter with the coming of summer.

A week later, Brzezinski met with Brown and Jones for what he described as a "very comprehensive review of the rescue plan." He came away convinced that the mission had a reasonable chance to succeed. Next, to gain support, he confided the outline of the rescue to Vice President Walter Mondale, Press Secretary Jody Powell, and White House Chief of Staff Hamilton Jordan. All three shared Brzezinski's concern over the increasing public pressure for more forthright action against Khomeini. It is likely that Brzezinski, with the help of his three colleagues, arranged for Carter to listen to a full briefing of the proposed rescue.

On 22 March 1980, only one month away from D-day, in the wooded, informal atmosphere of Camp David, Carter received his senior advisors. Present were Vance, Mondale, Brown, Turner, Jones, Powell, Brzezinski, and Aaron. After

General Jones described in detail how the rescue would be accomplished, Vance, according to his own and Brzezinski's account, advised against any military action, an opinion that Carter tacitly dismissed. While he did not directly authorize the raid, the president, at least, approved the covert, on-site inspection of Desert One by a reconnaissance plane with a three-person crew. Although he may not have acknowledged it to himself or others at the time, Carter had taken a major step toward his final decision.[3]

As he recalls in his memoirs, Carter was informed that on 31 March 1980, after a long flight, a plane (probably sponsored by the CIA) had landed at Desert One. The pilots reported that the place was "ideal." In the president's words, the landing surface was smooth, firm, and distant from towns, although there was a "seldom used country road nearby." (That characterization of the road was debatable.) Reportedly, while the crew obtained soil samples and planted remote-control beacons to guide incoming aircraft, which probably took an hour or so, six vehicles drove by, but the occupants evidently remained unaware of the agents' presence. Noting the number of vehicles, the Holloway investigators believed that the site carried more risk than General Vaught had assessed:

> The vehicles and helicopters abandoned along the road would more likely draw attention to the scene and ultimately to the C-130 wheel ruts. As a result COMJTF [Vaught] was on the horns of a dilemma: the risk of compromise was increased if the mission proceeded and was certain if the force withdrew. Clearly, another site away from roads would have markedly reduced compromising the mission in its early phases.

Yet a search for an alternate site would consume precious time, and there was no certainty that one would be found. So the planners accepted the odds and decided on Desert One. Holloway's investigators acknowledged that the decision, which must have received JCS approval, may have represented the only reasonable choice, but they insisted that the degree of risk associated with Desert One was not accurately calculated. More prudent planners, it can be argued, would have rejected Desert One on the basis that telltale signs would have been left near a well-traveled road. As the rescue force would have been spending almost two days in Iran, such detection could have blown its cover and wrecked the operation.[4]

Carter Grasps the Nettle

Fourteen days before the actual date of execution, Brzezinski reminded Carter that it was useless to continue negotiations with Khomeini. Unless something was done, he said, the American people would have to resign themselves to continued imprisonment of the hostages. Brzezinski urged that a rescue be conducted simultaneously with a "retaliatory strike [to] provide a broader context" in the event of a failed rescue attempt. Obviously persuaded, the president moved fast. On 7 April 1980, the United States severed diplomatic relations with Iran. Simultaneously Carter announced that he was committed to the safe return of the hostages and the preservation of national honor. With these words, he gave a warning sign to Khomeini and indirectly assured the American people that he would not tolerate a stalemate.[5]

On 11 April 1980, at a meeting of the National Security Council, Carter informed his advisors that he had authorized the rescue mission. He also remarked that President Anwar Sadat of Egypt, whom he held in high regard, had warned him that the United States's international standing was suffering from "excessive passivity," a euphemism for a lack of action. Brzezinski reports that Carter had received advice from his wife, Rosalynn, Mondale, Jordan, and Powell before deciding.

In his *Times* article, Brzezinski reported that a "grim-faced" president informed the National Security Council that the national honor was at stake and that "we ought to go ahead [with the rescue] without delay." On learning from General Jones that 24 April 1980 was the earliest the operation could begin, the president set that day for the rescue.[6]

At the meeting on 11 April Brzezinski took the floor in

support of the president's decision, urging that it was time to "lance the boil." The council members then discussed the question whether U.S. forces (presumably carrier aircraft) should conduct a concurrent, retaliatory strike in conjunction with the rescue. But Carter shunned the proposal, possibly because of the consequences—both international and domestic—that would be caused by the inevitable loss of lives. In rebuttal, Defense Secretary Harold Brown and CIA Director Stansfield Turner made clear that a simultaneous, punitive operation would help preserve the United States's international stature if the rescue effort fell apart.

Carter, still uncertain of the end result, put off his decision by directing the planners to devise an alternate plan to the punitive strike that he would consider and possibly approve at a later date. On 23 April, the day before D-day, Carter put the matter to rest by ruling out a concurrent air strike. According to Brzezinski, the president reasoned that such an attack would only complicate the rescue and exacerbate U.S. relations abroad. Officers in the Pentagon were mystified that the president had waited until the very day before the rescue operation to decide.[7]

Vance the Naysayer

As the only dissenter to the rescue plan, Secretary of State Vance made a final effort to block the operation. At a meeting of the National Security Council held on 15 April, Vance argued that the raid should be cancelled. Although he admitted he did not know when the hostages would be released, Vance predicted that any covert mission almost certainly would cause loss of life. He warned that even if the rescue force freed some of the hostages, the Iranians could simply capture American journalists in Iran and some two hundred other Americans living in Iran. He contended that the hostages were valuable to Khomeini only so long as they were not abused. Despite Brzezinski's proposal for direct military action, Vance insisted, "the more we declared our fear for their safety and our determination to leave no stone unturned to gain their freedom, the greater became their value to Khomeini." His solemn plea was made in vain.

In retrospect, Vance's evaluation was justified. Carter's critics argued that he should have sensed that the Iranians' threat to destroy all the hostages immediately was pure bluff.[8] The secretary of state later admitted that the Carter administration had contributed to Iran's exploitation of the situation by making it appear that the release of the hostages was the only concern of the government. Without the hostages alive, some argued, Iran would lose its psychological grip on the troubled Carter.

Other foreign experts, according to a *New York Times* writer, believed that a policy of ignoring or deemphasizing the crisis would have caused Iran to lose interest in holding the hostages. These political officers and Iranian specialists recommended that the United States should "tighten the screws." A year later, Carter admitted to second thoughts on the raid. Interviewed at his home in Plains, Georgia, he said that he "had thought a lot" about the aborted mission. He acknowledged that "when the press was excluded from Iran, I think the issue would have died down a lot more if I had decided to ignore the fate of the hostages or if I had decided just to stop any statements on the subject. That may have been the best approach."[9]

Helicopters to the Indian Ocean

The transfer of eight Sea Stallion helicopters to a carrier in the Indian Ocean, without breaking security, went off smoothly and exemplified service cooperation at its best. Reportedly, General Vaught's staff began the transport of helos and their maintenance crews in Air Force C-5 planes to Diego Garcia in the Indian Ocean during November 1979.

Over the past twenty years, this small British-owned island has been turned into a first-rate logistics base, shared jointly by the U.S. and the Royal navies. It is safe to assume that while at Diego Garcia, maintenance crews removed minesweeping gear from the aircraft and installed additional

Six of the eight helicopters assigned to the Tehran rescue operation are shown here on 5 February 1980 practicing formation flying near the USS *Nimitz* in the Indian Ocean. The helos were transferred from Helicopter Mine-Counter-measures Squadron 16 for the mission. (U.S. Navy)

fuel tanks for the long flight to Desert One. The modifications completed, it was a simple matter for the helicopters to be transferred at night to a carrier anchored off Diego Garcia. The carrier may then have sailed for a rendezvous with a second carrier some hundred miles at sea, where a second transfer could have taken place.

In late November, according to *Aviation Week*, six Sea Stallions appeared on board the carrier *Kitty Hawk*, one of two flattops in the Indian Ocean fleet. *Aviation Week* also stated that

The 92,000-ton USS *Nimitz*. This nuclear-powered behemoth, shown here with combat aircraft on deck, served as the mobile base for the eight RH-53 helicopters assigned to the rescue operation. (U.S. Navy)

in January 1980, these aircraft were transferred (at sea?) to the nuclear-powered *Nimitz*, newly arrived from the United States.[10] In any event, while the *Nimitz* was cruising on station in the Indian Ocean, the crew awoke one morning to find the helicopters on board. The chances are that the ship was no-where near Diego Garcia when the helos landed on its flight

The day before the mission, Colonel Charles Pitman, USMC (at right), confers with Captain Jack Batzler, commanding officer of the *Nimitz* (at left), and Colonel James Keating, USAF (center), a staff officer from the Pacific Command at Pearl Harbor. They are stand-ing in the hangar bay. (U.S. Navy)

The flight deck of the *Nimitz* on 24 April 1980. Rear Admiral Robert E. Kirksey (center, in jacket), commander Strike Force, Seventh Fleet, briefs pilots and crewmen prior to takeoff. With him are Colonel Charles Pitman, USMC, task force deputy commander for helicopters under General Vaught (third from right), and Lieutenant Commander Jack Ahart, USN (third from left). (U.S. Navy)

The hangar deck of the USS *Nimitz* in the Indian Ocean shortly before the start of the rescue mission on 24 April 1980. Crew members reposition a Navy RH-53 helicopter. (U.S. Navy)

deck. Two additional Sea Stallions already were on board, making a total of eight. Four days before the mission-launch, helicopter pilots and aircrews of Vaught's force reportedly were flown on board to join the detachment.

Naturally, the officers and men of the *Nimitz* sensed that a special operation was under way. The newly arrived pilots and aircrews were berthed in separate compartments but took their meals with the ship's company. In the wardroom, the newcomers observed civilities, sat down for meals, but avoided any conversation with the ship's officers. Security also extended to the hangar deck and flight deck, where no unauthorized persons were allowed.

There is every indication that the helos were carefully maintained by naval technicians and given test flights as needed. If a particular spare part had to be procured from Subic Bay or Pearl Harbor or the United States, a plane could deliver it on board in short order. Expert technicians (tech reps) from the Sikorski Division of United Technologies were on board to solve any repair problem. Knowledgeable sources state that in order to maintain a near-perfect performance level a test pilot and *two* naval maintenance crews were attached to each helicopter.[11] They further state that the original commander of the navy's minesweeping squadron, which had furnished the eight helos, was sent to the Indian Ocean (Diego Garcia?) to prepare his helos for the mission. He was accompanied by three of his best pilots and a number of squadron mechanics to help in the maintenance.

The helicopters were probably kept on the carrier's hangar deck well out of sight of Soviet intelligence-collection ships and satellites. As a result, the helicopters reportedly were flown only fifteen or twenty hours from January to mid-April 1980, instead of the usual three hours every other day.

Beckwith later charged that the "choppers," when they were transferred to the *Nimitz*, were not accompanied "by any of our own [task force] maintenance people." He went on to state that "the carrier provided its own maintenance to the Sea Stallions" and that the carrier "mechanics and their officers had no idea what the choppers were going to be used for." His

D-day, 24 April 1980, in the Indian Ocean as crewmen wait to board their RH-53 Sea Stallion helicopter. A giant elevator brings the helo from the hangar deck to the flight deck of the *Nimitz*. A tractor tows the helo into position for takeoff to Desert One. (U.S. Navy)

conclusion was that the helicopters would have been better served if their "own mechanics" had maintained them. The evidence seems irrefutable, however, that the aircraft were kept in top operating condition for the flight to Desert One. But, as sometimes happens in military operations, unexpected mishaps wrecked the crews' unstinting efforts.[12]

Interestingly, Washington was forced to reveal details of the top-secret plan to Britain's Prime Minister Margaret Thatcher, all because of an alert British official in Oman. Alarmed by the presence of American C-130s flying in and out of Masirah, an island in the Arabian Sea off Oman, this officer radioed London that U.S. forces might be preparing to aid Afghan freedom fighters in their war against the Soviet army. When queried by the British government, the Carter administration promptly sent Deputy Secretary of State Warren Christopher to London to disclose the rescue plan and request secrecy. Christopher was successful, for Prime Minister Thatcher, during the period before the raid, declined to answer unfriendly parliamentary questions relating to Diego Garcia and U.S. use of the base. The official silence observed by Britain was precisely that kind of cooperation expected from a longtime ally.[13]

Carter's Concern over Casualties

On the evening of 16 April 1980, the task force leaders, dressed in casual clothes, met with the president in the White House Situation Room to brief him on Eagle Claw, the code name of the rescue mission. In his memoirs, Carter writes that he was particularly impressed with the presentations by Major General Vaught, Lieutenant General Gast, and Colonel Beckwith. The president quizzed them at length and received what he considered "satisfactory answers." However, the prospect of excessive fatalities was a matter of much concern to Carter. In the two-and-a-half-hour session, he impressed upon Vaught, Gast, and Beckwith that they were "under instructions not to harm innocent bystanders and to avoid bloodshed whenever possible."[14]

In Brzezinski's account of the briefing, Carter was emphatic that "every effort be made to avoid wanton killings." The president even went so far as to instruct General Jones to devote his personal attention to the matter. Any notion of wanton killings (outlawed by the laws of war) should have played no part in the planning.

Concern over excessive casualties did not square with Colonel Beckwith's recollection: "He [President Carter] looked at me and said, 'Use that necessary force to get our Americans out of the Embassy and back to this country.'" Beckwith goes on to say, "When we went into that Embassy, it was our aim to kill all Iranian guards—the people holding our hostages—and we weren't going in there to arrest them; we were going in there to shoot them right between the eyes, and to do it with vigor!" So that no one would be in doubt as to his meaning, Beckwith continued: "We intended to kill 'em. We certainly intended to . . . about the guards . . . he's my adversary and I'm certainly not going up to him and shake his hand. I'm going to blow him away!"

Beckwith, in his book, reveals that Deputy Secretary of State Warren Christopher seemed upset to learn that his men were prepared to kill Iranians. Beckwith anticipated that during the assault twenty to twenty-five guards would be on duty. If they were armed, "they were all to be taken out." He also knew that during the raid a U.S. hostage might overpower a guard and take his weapon. If Beckwith's men saw *anyone* with a weapon, they were trained to kill the individual; there would be no time for recognition of any hapless American holding a gun in the shadows. The paradox is that Carter believed the lives of the hostages to be paramount; yet he had authorized a raid in which there was a good possibility that some of them might die.

Despite his graphic choice of words, Beckwith's reasoning coincided with military doctrine. A combat commander, on being assigned a military objective, is expected to attain it in timely fashion and, in so far as possible, with a minimum of casualties to his own men. Critics charged that the president appeared not to realize that he could not have it both ways. If he were upset by the awful possibility of Beckwith's men inflicting too many casualties, he should have canceled the raid. Otherwise, they argued, he would be sending men into an action where they might hesitate to shoot first—hardly good practice in a life-or-death confrontation with the enemy.[15]

Carter was also conscious of the possibilities of casualties at Manzariyeh, the final departure point for the rescue party and the hostages. For some time Beckwith had been urging that fighter support be available on short notice. He had pointed out to his seniors that it made no sense to rescue the hostages, place them on board C-141 Starlifters, and then have them wiped out by an Iranian fighter pilot lucky enough to spot the U.S. planes and rescue team. At the White House briefing he again brought up the need for air support. The president resolved the issue by giving the order, "There will be air cover from Manzariyeh all the way out of Iran."[16]

In sum, the actors included a president anxious to avoid any semblance of an uncertain procrastinator; a pugnacious but militarily unqualified national security advisor pressing for covert action to rescue the hostages; a cautious secretary of state who anticipated trouble if the military rescue went forward; a defense secretary whose role in the entire affair remains vague; a chairman of the Joint Chiefs of Staff under pressure to keep the operation small and, above all, secret; a distinguished combat general expected to organize and train a multiservice force for a highly complicated operation to be launched in the shortest possible time, but to avoid much killing; and last, a highly competent helicopter commander and an equally distinguished commando officer whose recommendation for a minimum of nine helicopters had been turned down, a decision that augured ill for the mission.

4

The Flight of the Luckless Helicopters

Preparations at Qena

Any undercover operation requires deception—not only of enemies but sometimes of friends as well. Thus, the government of Oman, whose base at Masirah was to be used for refueling the C-130s, was not told the true nature of the mission, simply because permission to refuel probably would not have been granted. Nor was Egyptian president Anwar Sadat, who agreed to the use of an airbase by the C-130s and the rescue force, informed that Tehran was the target, although he may have guessed it.[1]

On 20 April, Beckwith's Green Berets, based at Fort Bragg, N.C., were airlifted from the United States via Frankfurt, West Germany, to the airbase at Qena, Egypt, where General Vaught had set up his command post. Here they remained in seclusion for several days. A detailed account published in the *Washington Post* two years later reports that eighty-three Army Rangers also departed at the same time from Hunter Army Airfield near Savannah, Georgia. The Rangers were to secure the airfield at Desert One and, later, at Manzariyeh.

Colonel Charlie A. Beckwith, leader of the assault team that was to storm the U.S. Embassy compound in Tehran to rescue the hostages. Left with only five helicopters at Desert One (one less than the plan called for), Beckwith recommended that the mission be aborted. He is shown here in November 1981 at the White House ceremony welcoming home the hostages who were released through negotiation. (Wide World Photos)

Beckwith's Delta team met the Rangers in a shelter that they named Bunker 13. According to the *Post*, the Deltas were dressed in nondescript clothes, a ruse that would help in their escape from Iran if the operation went awry. Untypically, they wore blue jeans, flak vests, black army jackets, combat boots, and navy watchcaps (a blue-wool toque). Sewn on each jacket sleeve was a small U.S. flag covered with tape. After they had stormed the embassy, they were to tear off the tape, exposing the flag. When loaded with weapons and his pack, each soldier weighed in at about 270 pounds.

The 120 men to be airlifted from Desert One to Desert Two included 93 Delta men, 2 Iranian generals who would serve as interpreters, drivers and assistant drivers for the ride from Desert Two to Tehran, and a 13-man Special Forces team to rescue the three American diplomats held at the Ministry of Foreign Affairs. For security reasons, this unit had prepared in West Germany for the operation. One of the assistant drivers was Navy Captain John A. Butterfield, who was a faculty member of the U.S. Naval Academy. Fluent in Farsi, he had volunteered, as had all others on the mission.[2]

The Deltas reportedly were armed with a variety of weapons including German HK-21 burp guns, M79 and M203 grenade launchers, handguns, MP5 submachine guns, M60 machine guns, and C4 plastic high-explosive charges. They carried yellow plastic thongs for use as handcuffs. They did not wear steel helmets, which are heavy, tend to obscure the vision, and are not suited for swift, stealthy assaults in the night. Eash man was "sanitized" before the operation to ensure that he carried only a military identification card and tags.

The soldiers saw the two gunships on the ground at Qena. Modified Hercules transports equipped with machine guns and small, rapid-fire cannon, the planes were to fly "shotgun" over the embassy compound's fourteen buildings on twenty-seven acres. If so ordered, the crew was to spray mobs with gunfire. The other gunship was to patrol the area above Tehran airport, preventing any combat planes from taking off. These lethal aircraft had been developed for use in

Vietnam, where they had proved their fighting value.[3] If the
success of the operation depended on air support, Beckwith
would have called in the gunships. In this event, the death toll
of Iranians might well have been in the hundreds.

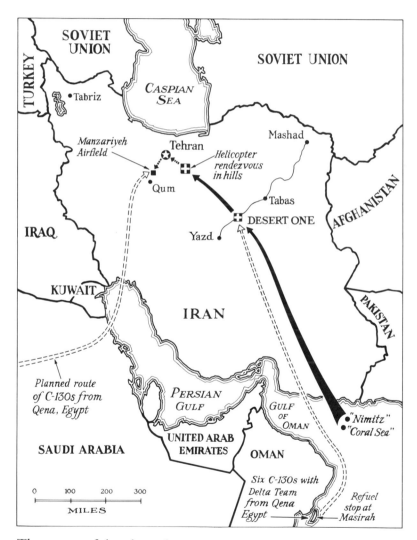

The routes of the planned rescue.

In the few hours remaining at Qena, the assault force, we are told, was briefed once more on the plan. Plastic maps showing details of the attack were distributed. Officers reviewed the techniques of escape-and-evasion (E-and-E). If the assault failed, the men were to head overland to Turkey. To draw the attention of U.S. intelligence officers who would be monitoring satellite cameras, the escaping soldiers reportedly were to form huge alphabet letters with stones or vegetation that would show up on the film. Each man would carry a compass, map, U.S. and Iranian money, strobe lights, and a Farsi phrase book.

Having learned only the night before of the exact location of the hostages inside the embassy compound, the Delta team boarded two C-141 transports on 24 April and flew southward to Masirah Island off the east coast of Oman, where they refueled. That evening they departed in C-130s for Desert One, refueling in the air from KC-135 tankers.[4]

Bad Luck and Black BIMs

The helicopter phase of the operation began at 7:30 P.M. on 24 April, when eight Sea Stallions rose in succession from the *Nimitz*, cruising in the Arabian Sea. Assuming quickly a loose diamond formation, they began their fateful flight of six hundred miles to the rendezvous. That afternoon the pilots had been briefed on the weather. The meteorologists had made a long-range prediction that good weather would prevail during the flight to Desert One. As the Holloway report put it, "The probability of VMC [visual meteorological conditions] for the helicopter ingress was reasonably high." It went on to say that Vaught's force "was comfortable that the weather would not be a limiting factor for mission success because of the predicted high frequency of VMC along the helicopter route."

On the other hand, General Jones stated in his report that every effort was made to duplicate in training the conditions that the helicopter crews could encounter on the mission, such as reduced visibility because of fog or no moonlight. The

On the evening of 24 April 1980, the eight Sea Stallion helicopters lift off from the *Nimitz*'s flight deck (longer than three football fields). At the left is the ship's bridge structure, the "island." The figure in the foreground is a flight director. (U.S. Navy)

mission planners had not, however, envisioned the worst possible case—a blinding, giant dust cloud. Once the helicopters entered the dust cloud en route to Desert One, all ground navigational points were partially or completely hidden, forcing the pilots to fly on instruments. Perhaps the limited training period prevented more training in flight under no visibility. Whatever the reason, the investigators found that the helicopter pilots were not prepared for the protracted instrument flying encountered on the mission.

Back on the carrier *Nimitz* some hours before takeoff, an accident caused a minor flap. An enlisted man, working on the hangar deck, mistakenly opened a fire-fighting system, which threw a spray of chemically treated foam on five helicopters. Crewmen quickly washed down the aircraft with fresh water and checked all electric circuits and working parts. The aircraft suffered no damage and none of the subsequent matériel failures was traced to the wetting.[5]

Once in the air, the pilots flew low to take advantage of the mountainous terrain, which masked them from Iranian radar. This tactic proved successful, for the Iranians had no inkling that U.S. aircraft were invading their territory.

Almost two hours into the flight across the desert, a cockpit warning light in helo 6 flashed a signal of a possible rotor blade failure. This signal, known as a BIM (blade inspection method), forced the pilot to land and inspect the rotor. The pilot in number 8 helo saw number 6 land (recall that no radio communication was permitted), broke formation, and landed alongside the stricken craft. To their great disappointment, the crew found that the BIM instrument indicated a loss of nitrogen within the hollow blade, a casualty known as a "black BIM." The pilot decided not to attempt to fly the aircraft. Unfortunately, neither the electrical system that transmitted the warning to the cockpit nor the BIM device itself could with certainty reveal if the trouble lay in a possible blade crack or not. If the blade were in fact cracked and the helo were to take off, then the crew stood a good chance of crashing. The possibility that this black BIM might well have been a faulty signal received the Holloway group's critical attention. At issue was the strong suspicion that Vaught's staff might not have sufficiently researched the occurrence of faulty BIM signals. The Holloway panel found that in some 38,000 flight runs of RH-53D helicopters *not one* crack had been found in a rotor blade, despite three BIM signals. If this research had been carried out before the mission, the results could conceivably have caused the pilot to ignore the BIM light and fly on to Desert One.

The crew of helo 6 removed all classified material, abandoned the aircraft, boarded helo 8, and resumed the flight. Had the marines blown up number 6, the explosion and flames might have set off an alert that could have jeopardized the entire mission.

"Flying in a Bowl of Milk"

Three hours after takeoff, the seven remaining helicopters, still in their diamond formation and cruising at low altitude, flew unexpectedly into a huge dust cloud. Maintaining flight formation became impossible; pilots separated and were forced for some two hours to fly on instruments to maintain course and altitude. One pilot recalled that it was like "flying in a bowl of milk." Another source described the cloud as composed of fine talcum-like powder that sifted into the aircraft, raising the cockpit temperature from 88° to 93°. Although they did not know it, the pilots had encountered what is known in Arabic as a *haboob*.

Meanwhile, because he believed that the dust cloud might "blow past," Lieutenant Colonel Seiffert, the pilot of helicopter 1, landed his aircraft. He was followed by his wingman in helicopter 2. Using a special radio channel that had minimal chance of interception by Iranian listening posts, Seiffert as the flight leader informed General Vaught, back at his base at Qena, that despite the dust it was possible for the helicopters to press on. Vaught then ordered the flight to do so. Vaught was still unaware, as were Colonel Pitman, Lieutenant Colonel Seiffert, and Colonel Beckwith, that helo 6 was down.[6]

One hour later, the widely separated helicopters emerged in the clear. The relief felt by the aircrews was

Lieutenant Colonel Edward R. Seiffert, USMC, flight leader of the eight helicopters that took off from the aircraft carrier *Nimitz* for a rendezvous with the rescue force in the Iranian desert. Three of the helicopters suffered mechanical failures en route, and the mission was aborted. (Buffalo *News*)

THOMAS COOPER LIBRARY
UNIVERSITY OF SOUTH CAROLINA
COLUMBIA, S. C. 29208

short-lived, for the good visibility lasted only an hour. Ahead lay a second cloud even thicker than the first. It was later estimated that the cloud spread 200 miles across the desert to an altitude of 6,000 feet. Although task force weather officers knew of the possibility of dust clouds, this information never reached the helicopter pilots who might encounter them. Because of the emphasis on security, the traditional relationship between pilots and weather forecasters had been severed to preserve secrecy.[7]

The Holloway investigation disclosed that Vaught's weather team had identified hazardous weather, including suspended dust, which the pilots might encounter on the mission. The weather annex of the operations plan contained a table showing by location and month the frequency of suspended-dust appearances. Yet both the helicopter and C-130 pilots later testified, according to the Holloway report, that they had not been informed of this phenomenon. For reasons of security, the pilots were not shown the operations plan with its weather annex.

In probing the reason for withholding vital weather data from the pilots, the panel concluded that although the phenomenon of suspended dust occurs frequently in the Iranian desert, but does not often affect settlements, it, therefore, is usually not recorded. If the planners had been fully aware of the high risk of relying on limited weather data, they might have taken a different approach. Unfortunately, because of compartmentation, the weather team rarely—if ever—talked to the pilots. Most of the time, an intelligence officer—not a meteorology officer—conveyed weather information to the pilots. But if the pilots, the forecasters, and the weather researchers had been permitted direct conversation, the matter of the dust phenomenon might have surfaced and been resolved. If the pilots had been warned of the possibility of encountering suspended dust, they would have been better prepared to make tactical decisions.[8]

There remains the final question of why the dust clouds were not forecast in the pilots' preflight weather briefing. It is not always possible to predict dust clouds with accuracy. The masses that lay over the flight path of the helicopters were probably caused by a huge downwash of turbulent air generated by thunderstorms fifty miles to the west of the helicopters' course. Furthermore, weather satellites, in 1980 at least, were not capable of producing accurate and timely imagery of dust clouds, according to the Holloway report and *Aerospace Daily*. The failure of Vaught's staff to brief the pilots on the possibility of haboobs in order to preserve security was a costly lesson. Future planners undoubtedly will think twice before they alter the flow of information and the longtime liaison between weathermen and pilots.[9]

As the helicopters battled their way toward Desert One, an alarm signal flashed in helo 5, which carried Colonel Pitman. A motor that operated a blower for cooling air to the aircraft power supply had overheated and failed. This casualty, in turn, rendered navigation and flight control systems inoperative or erratic. The trouble, allegedly, was traced to a crew member who had placed a flak jacket and duffel bag over the cooling vent, causing the motor to burn out.

Within a few minutes the loss of flight instruments, combined with poor visibility and vertigo, convinced the pilots that they should return to base. The crew knew that they were about thirty minutes away from a range of mountains that had to be crossed. Uncertain that the helicopter could climb above the range and not wishing to risk detection of their flight by Iranian radar, Colonel Pitman reluctantly aborted the mission. Unfortunately, because of radio silence, Colonel Pitman had no way of knowing that helo 6 was already down or that in a few more minutes he would have broken into the clear. In another fifty-five minutes he would have arrived at Desert One. The decision to return to the *Nimitz* reduced the number of helicopters to six, the absolute minimum needed by Colonel Beckwith to move out from Desert One to Desert Two.[10]

General Vaught learned of the abort after the pilot, on reaching the Indian Ocean, broke radio silence to notify the

The commander of the helicopter detachment, Colonel Charles H. Pitman, USMC
(shown here as a brigadier general, the rank
which he later attained). A casualty to the
cooling system for navigational instruments
in helicopter 5, combined with poor visibility
and a lack of radio communication, caused
Colonel Pitman to return to the carrier
Nimitz. (U.S. Navy)

ship that he was low on fuel. Presumably Pitman could communicate only with the *Nimitz* and relied on the ship to radio Vaught and Beckwith. The carrier's skipper immediately changed course and raced to meet the stricken helo. The sanitized log of the *Nimitz* shows that shortly after midnight and some five hours after the helos had taken off, the ship turned from an easterly course to a northwest track toward the coast. The captain was on the bridge and remained there until 3:03 A.M., close to the time the last C-130 had lifted off from Desert One.[11]

Meanwhile, pilots of the six remaining helicopters grimly concentrated on their instruments as they navigated through the white dust. About one hundred miles from Desert One, they broke out into clear weather and straggled in to the airstrip some fifty to eighty-five minutes late. More delay could have been a reason to cancel the mission, simply because so few hours of darkness remained.[12]

The Cost of Unnecessary Radio Silence

The imposition of radio silence, a consequence of the heavy emphasis on security, choked off communications during the actual operation. Strict radio silence discouraged the exchange of vital operational reports when the unexpected happened. Probing into the reason the pilot of helo 5 abandoned his mission, the Holloway investigators found that overly tight transmission restrictions had prevented the lead C-130 from passing weather information to the helicopters. The pilot later acknowledged that he probably would have continued his flight if he had only known that he was within twenty-five minutes of exiting the dust cloud. Nor did the helicopter flight leader, Lieutenant Colonel Seiffert, know of helo 5's abort. The failure of helo 5 to arrive at the rendezvous, noted the review group, proved pivotal because one more helicopter might have permitted the mission to continue.[13]

Sadly, there were technical means to enable the transmission of information to the C-130s and to helicopters enroute without likelihood of compromising the mission. Such transmissions, the panel asserted, would have meant a "covered [protected] and secure flow of vital information to the rescue force while en route to Desert One." These are damaging words. They suggest that senior decision makers in the White House and Pentagon did not appreciate the degree of security afforded by certain communication channels or how to use these channels to best advantage. Conceding that operational security was critical to achieving surprise, the panel nevertheless maintained that use of available and appropriate radio equipment would not have damaged security. Failure to use it, on the other hand, meant that information essential for informed command decisions was stifled.[14] It can in fact be said that the imposed silence on radio transmission was an underlying cause of the mission's collapse.

General Vaught and his officers were among the best in the armed forces, but the undertaking was bound to suffer if the task force commander could not receive timely information, if his subcommanders could not be made aware of sudden changes, or if men and aircraft could not be repositioned as the tactical picture changed. General Vaught's force achieved communications security, but at too high a price.

Clearly, the helicopter pilots would have had a better chance of reaching Desert One if someone had given more thought to the axiom that communication is always risky in war. It was the planners' job to reduce the risk by identifying such uncertainties and dealing with them. The Holloway panel put its collective finger on the basic weakness displayed by Vaught's staff: his planners were not sufficiently sensitive to those "areas of great uncertainty" that might have had (and, in fact, did have) a shattering impact on the rescue mission.[15]

The Missing Pathfinder Planes

Admiral Holloway and his colleagues found another oversight in the operational plan that contributed to the mission's miscarriage. This mishap stemmed from the failure to furnish the helo pilots with advance weather information along their route, which could have been obtained by a C-130 pathfinder (guide plane). It was pure conjecture, the panel conceded, but if General Vaught had possessed an advance weather report from a C-130, he might have balanced it against his knowledge of the training of the pilots under visual flight conditions and ordered an abort. Then after a day or two, he could have resumed operations when the weather had cleared.[16] Used as a pathfinder, the C-130 might have burned up more fuel, but such consumption would have been balanced by the probability that the helos would have burned less fuel by arriving on time. They therefore would have fueled faster at Desert One, extending the precious night cover.

In the armed forces, long-range aircraft are a proved and often-used means of collecting accurate weather reports over unknown areas where there is high risk. The panel members asked why the task force staff had not arranged for a weather reconnaissance plane to scout the helicopter route. They were told, first, that the possibilities for visual-flight weather for the helicopters were excellent and, second, that such a flight would have been "one more sortie" that could have alerted the Iranians and endangered the mission. Excessive regard for security was sufficient to deter "what appeared to be a simple and straightforward approach to handling unexpected weather conditions," said the panel.[17]

General Vaught and the weather officers had at hand the planes to obtain more timely and accurate weather data. As the panel saw it, a pilot on weather reconnaissance would have seen the dust clouds, reported the size, and assessed the chances of the helicopters' navigating through them.

Evidence suggests further that the helicopters may not have been completely equipped for a 600-nautical-mile, low-visibility flight over unknown desert and mountain ranges. In fact, Admiral Holloway's investigators found the helicopters to be "austerely prepared," a term implying that they were not equipped with state-of-the-art instruments. For example, the helos were not fitted with terrain-following radar (TFR) or forward-looking infrared (FLIR), a device providing extended night vision to the pilots. The pilots, when flying in visual meteorological condition (VMC), were chiefly dependent on what aviators call "Mark I eyeball," that is, their own visual acuity aided by night-vision goggles (NVGs).

While investigation revealed that the aircraft were equipped with the precision-inertial navigation system (PINS) and a long-range, electronic navigation system known as OMEGA, the crew had "received only limited training [in the system] and expressed low confidence in the equipment and their ability to employ it." As a consequence, the pilots planned to rely heavily on dead reckoning (DR), that is, a method of navigation using direction by compass and the amount of distance made good from the last known position. Although the pilots navigated safely to Desert One, their performance would have been more effective if a pathfinder had been used.

In sum, senior planners gave too much weight to the favorable weather predictions and too little to the idea of using a pathfinder. Panel members concluded that if one or two C-130 pathfinders had been used, they would have increased the probability of all helicopters (except helo 6) arriving at Desert One. Reluctant to point a collective, accusing finger, the investigators, nevertheless, found that "provisions for handling weather conditions could and should have been enhanced."

5

The Crash at Desert One

Heavy Traffic at the Airstrip

The first C-130 arrived at Desert One about 10 P.M. On board
were Colonel Beckwith, some of his Delta Force, and Colonel
James Kyle, USAF, whom General Vaught had named as the
on-scene commander for the desert rendezvous. Circling the
field, the pilot landed on his third time around. On the plane
were the combat control team charged with the control of air
traffic after Desert One was secured, and the road watch team
which was responsible for securing the field and posting pa-
trols around the perimeter. These special teams included
Rangers and some Delta Force support personnel.

Once the wheels stopped rolling, the road watch team
swiftly off-loaded a jeep and spread out to block the two road
approaches to the strip. They were none too soon, for a large
Mercedes bus was headed toward them. The startled driver
ignored the command to halt, stopping only after shots were
fired over and under the bus. The Rangers then took into
custody forty-five terrified Iranians who must have viewed
the Americans as men from outer space. The stunned passengers quickly heeded the words of a Farsi-speaking agent who

told them that if they were quiet no harm would come to them.[1]

Minutes later, another unit of the road watch team spotted a small fuel truck. Again the drivers ignored orders to halt. One of the Rangers fired an antitank rocket, setting the fuel truck on fire, whereupon the driver jumped out and ran a hundred yards back to a pickup truck which had not been spotted by the road watch team. The pickup made a U-turn, picked up the bus driver, and escaped amid a hail of bullets. An anonymous C-130 crewman later wrote that the fiercely burning fuel truck nearly blinded his pilot just as the plane was on its final approach. Fortunately, the pilot was able to land the plane without mishap. Any fears that the escaped truck drivers would alert the Iranian authorities were discounted by Colonel Beckwith, who believed them to be gasoline smugglers. If so, the chances were good that they mistook the raiders for local police on patrol.

At about this stage, Beckwith radioed a report to General Vaught, who passed it on to the Pentagon. Jimmy Carter writes that he approved Beckwith's recommendation that all forty-five Iranians be flown to Egypt by C-130; they would be returned to Iran after the operation. Beckwith, in contrast, writes in *Delta Force* that such a contingency had been foreseen and a plan prepared to haul any inadvertent witnesses out by C-130.[2] As matters turned out, these harmless civilians remained at Desert One.

Within the next two hours the first two C-130s to land had discharged the rescue force and departed. Meanwhile, four more C-130s, three of them loaded with fuel, had landed and were parked. The Delta team was positioned on the ground ready to be flown to Desert Two. Aircrews had wrestled fuel hoses from the aircraft for the fueling operation. Yet the helicopters had not arrived, and with each passing minute Kyle and Beckwith became more uneasy.

Finally, fifty-five minutes behind schedule, the first helicopter landed. As each helo arrived, its rotors blasted dust from the ground. Amid the noise, refueling proceeded slowly, and confusion was compounded by the absence of an identifiable command post for Colonel Kyle, who also lacked runners (messengers). Furthermore, because backup radios were not carried in the first two C-130s to land, Kyle was not guaranteed secure radio communications until the arrival of the third C-130.[3]

Unhappily, no one had foreseen that deafening noise and swirling dust would make command and communication at Desert One very difficult. None of the key personnel (Kyle, Beckwith, and their deputies) wore any insignia or marks for easy recognition. Thus, when they issued orders to the marine pilots (who might not have seen them before), there were questions as to their identity. Subsequent testimony confirmed that staff planners were wrong in their belief that personal recognition between key officers would be adequate for the operation.

There were other deficiencies. Oddly enough, the task force had never exercised together in the western U.S. training area. Air Force officers later admitted that once they had landed at Desert One, they had seen immediately that the operation had taken on complexities which had not been envisioned during the training stage.

To make matters worse, each plane kept its engines turning over so that there would be no start-up failures in the event of an emergency takeoff. The roar of powerful turbojet engines not only made voice communication difficult, but in some places the dust kicked up by the blasts obscured the landscape so much that men and aircraft became shadowy figures.[4]

A crucial question was whether the C-130s should have kept their engines running continuously while on the airstrip. Each aircraft was powered by four Allison turboprop engines, each rated at 4,050 horsepower. The C-130 required no separate ground start-up power source because the pilot used on-board batteries for turn-up. Probably, if all engines had been shut down, each plane could have had four engines started within two minutes. Again, if each pilot had kept only one engine turning over, he would have had a ready power source for communications and other services. Equally important, the noise level would have been reduced sharply. But other factors were overriding. If the C-130s had shut down

Colonel James H. Kyle, USAF, commander of the C-130 transports and on-site commander at Desert One. Colonel Kyle was highly experienced in special operations. After the tragic collision, he ordered his force to board C-130s and return to Egypt. (U.S. Air Force)

some or all four engines, there was a danger that on start-up, an engine might "shear a starter shaft." Such a casualty, while remote, would have required a three-engine takeoff, which would have been much too risky. Therefore, C-130 pilots were told to keep all engines running, a seemingly prudent decision, as the planners had envisioned the circumstances.

Starting the helicopters was a different problem. The RH-53D usually required an exterior power unit to start its two engines. Lacking such units for Operation Eagle Claw, the helicopters carried special flasks of high-pressure air to turn over the engines. To save this limited air supply for use at Desert Two, the pilots, while at Desert One, were forced to keep their engines turning over. The net result was that a man had to shout directly in the ear of his listener to be understood.[5]

The Decision to Abort the Mission

At Desert One Beckwith stood poised for the biggest operation of his career. As he waited restlessly for the arrival of the helicopters, no one could fault him for his impatience. Success depended on absolute surprise; darkness was running out; and the situation did not look encouraging. At last, in Beckwith's words, "The first helicopter sits down . . . and then we wait and finally . . . all six choppers are there." Dawn would break at 5:30, so Beckwith had only a few hours of darkness to complete refueling and fly on to Desert Two before first light. From rehearsals during training, he knew that a helo could refuel in forty to seventy minutes, depending on the amount of fuel needed.[6]

The last two of the six helicopters finally arrived, eighty-five minutes late. Worse, one had sustained a mechanical defect that irrevocably sealed the fate of the mission. Two hours after departure from the carrier, the crew of helo 2 discovered that its hydraulic system was defective. Not until the aircraft landed could the men inspect the damage and ascertain that the hydraulic fluid in the second-stage system had leaked overboard. With no fluid, the hydraulic pump promptly froze. Once on the ground the crew traced the trouble to a crack in a jam nut located outside the crew space. No spare pump was at hand, and even if one had been available, the crew did not have time enough to install it.

Helo 2 did not crash en route to Desert One because the first-stage and second-stage hydraulic systems were separate systems, each capable of meeting all flight requirements. But when the first-stage failed, there was no back-up system. Consequently, if the second-stage failed, then a crash would be inevitable. The pilot understood his dangerous predicament but had to push on to Desert One, hoping that once there he might make repairs. His wish was in vain. The mission was now down to five helicopters, one below the required minimum.[7] If the crew and the task force leaders had been willing to risk catastrophic failure by flying on one hydraulic system, helo 2 could have continued the operation. They properly rejected this chancy option.

Colonel Beckwith received the first warning that he would have to abort from a marine pilot who climbed out of his aircraft and told him that "we are down to five helicopters." Later, at a Pentagon press conference, Beckwith recalled that the site commander, Colonel Kyle, confirmed this disappointing development, at which point Beckwith said: "Sir, my recommendation is that we abort . . . please tell me which aircraft you want me to load on, the 130s." Kyle said, "Would you consider taking five [helos] and going ahead, and think about it before you answer me." Beckwith replied, "I know that. Give me a couple of seconds to think it over. And I said to him by his first name [Jim] there's just no way." Asked why he needed six helicopters to complete the mission, Beckwith responded, "If we didn't have six, we wouldn't have ended up with two . . . I believed that we would lose two helos in the [soccer] stadium alone." In short, Beckwith expected more mechanical trouble and was determined to stick to his requirement of six helos.[8]

Kyle thereupon radioed General Vaught, who in turn called the Pentagon. Defense Secretary Brown passed the news on to President Carter, who approved the decision. As Carter tells it, he received notifications from Beckwith and Vaught recommending termination. The president wisely responded, "Let's go with his recommendation." Carter really had no other choice because Beckwith, the man on the spot, was the only person qualified to make the decision.[9]

Tension at the White House

After the helos had lifted off from the *Nimitz*, General Jones in the Pentagon phoned Brzezinski at the White House to report that the mission was under way and that the weather was good. Admiral Turner contributed the news that, thanks to last-minute intelligence, Beckwith's Deltas had been told the exact location of the hostages in the compound. Shortly thereafter, the White House was informed that only six helicopters had arrived at Desert One. General Jones did not know why the other two were delayed.

At 3:15 P.M., Washington time, Defense Secretary Brown telephoned to say that one helo had been abandoned in the desert and that the other had returned, "unauthorized," to the *Nimitz*. Minutes later, Carter learned that a busload of Iranians had been captured but that one vehicle (the pickup truck) had escaped after the driver had seen the aircraft and soldiers. At 3:30 P.M. General Jones advised the president to allow the mission to proceed.

Less than an hour later, while Brzezinski was talking to Vance and Ambassador Sol M. Linowitz on the Middle East situation, he was informed by Harold Brown that four helos had completed refueling and two were receiving fuel from C-130s (not quite an accurate report). In forty minutes, all aircraft would depart Desert One for the next phase. Bad news came only minutes later at 4:45 P.M., when Brown reported, "I think we have an abort situation." The flyable helicopters were now down to five. At this point, Brzezinski questioned Brown sharply. Why not go ahead with five? Brown reminded him that the plan called for a minimum of six. Brzezinski thereupon ordered him to review the situation with

General Jones and to get the opinion of Colonel Beckwith. If Beckwith believed he could carry on with five helos, then "I would back him all the way," Brzezinski said.

Brzezinski then interrupted the president, who was in conference, telling him privately of a possible abort. Brzezinski briefly considered (but resisted) pressing Carter to proceed with five helicopters in a "daring single stroke for the big prize." The president called for the recommendations of Vaught and Beckwith. Brown then advised the president that Beckwith was firm on a minimum of six, thus ending further discussion. Brzezinski subsequently wrote that he was "relieved" to learn that the "other senior officers" at Desert One were of like mind in aborting the mission. In fact, for Beckwith, the minimum of six helicopters had been set well before D-day.

Beckwith states in his book that when General Vaught, from his command post at Qena, asked him "to consider going with five [helicopters], he [Beckwith] lost respect right then for General Vaught." Beckwith was upset because the general knew that if the helicopters were reduced to five, the mission would abort. What Beckwith did not know was that the query to consider going ahead with five came from Brzezinski (presumably speaking for Carter) via Defense Secretary Brown, to General Jones, then Vaught, and finally to Beckwith. Vaught was unavoidably caught up in civilian meddling in a combat situation, a fact that Beckwith did not know.

Was It Possible to Proceed with Five Helos?

An officer, who had an insider's view of the operation, suggests that the eleventh-hour intelligence on the location of the hostages may have prompted the Joint Chiefs to consider carrying out the mission with five helicopters. It was only hours before Beckwith's move from Egypt to Desert One that a U.S. agent had learned from an embassy cook that all the hostages were locked in the embassy chancellery. Previously, Beckwith had assumed that they were spread among several buildings.

Should the Joint Chiefs, General Vaught, and Beckwith have explored the possibility that the concentration of the fifty-three Americans in one building warranted a reduction in the size of the assault force? Should Colonel Beckwith have considered returning one helicopter-load of troops from Desert One to Egypt in C-130s to allow the mission to continue with five helos? The sanitized version of the Holloway Report is silent on these points. Beckwith, in his book, *Delta Force*, relates how he changed his assault plan in light of the cook's report. On receipt of the news, he immediately reassigned eight men from his Blue team to the Red team, which was charged with rushing the chancellery. The Blue team was to "neutralize" the motor pool and the power plant. Knowing of Beckwith's dubious regard for the operational reliability of the helicopters, we may conclude that even if the thought had entered his mind, he would have dismissed it as impracticable.

Exploding Munitions and Blazing Aircraft

Meanwhile at Desert One, Colonel Kyle conferred with Lieutenant Colonel Seiffert on the disposition of the five flyable helicopters. On the latter's recommendation, Kyle directed that the aircraft be topped off with fuel and flown back to the *Nimitz*. In repositioning for fueling, helo 3, piloted by Major James Schaefer, lifted off the ground, creating great swirls of dust.[10] Witnesses testified that the helo moved left, then right, then banked to the right, crashing into a C-130. Flames shot up. The pilot of helo 4 (which was astern of helo 3) described the collision. "It resembled slow motion, like in the movies. First the wind, then the dust stirred, then a boiling sensation of fuel, fire, and pieces of the chopper." Sergeant Joseph L. Beyers, a crewman on the C-130 and one of the survivors, said, "We had all this dust coming down from the rotors and all our dust came right at them from our engines. . . . The helo pilot could not see." The time at Desert One was approximately 2:00 A.M.

Colonel Beckwith gave a graphic description of the smashup at a Pentagon press conference some days later. He

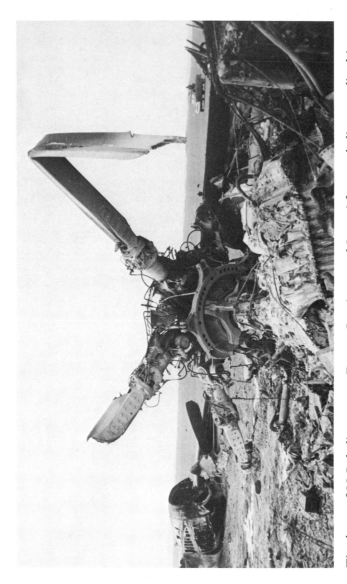

Wreckage of U.S. helicopters at Desert One in central Iran. After one helicopter sliced into a parked C-130 transport, the U.S. rescue force abandoned the scene, leaving behind eight American dead. The remaining helicopters were later destroyed by Iranian air force jets. (United Press International)

was sitting in a C-130 up forward when "all of a sudden a 130 exploded. It was one hell of a fire . . . a huge, mammoth fireball." A side door of the flaming C-130 served as an escape hatch for thirty-nine soldiers, some of whom were carried out. Some people asked why the troopers did not try to rescue all the men left in the burning C-130. The answer is that no one could have survived, said Beckwith, who compared the sight with a Fourth of July pyrotechnics display.

Five air force men in the cockpit of the C-130 perished in the flames, as did three marines in helo 3. Four army men suffered serious burns as they fled the burning C-130. Others risked their lives to rescue several unconscious men trapped on the ground near the plane. Sergeant Beyers, who had managed to crawl to an open door of the C-130, was catapulted out by the blast. Providentially, medics with the Delta team rendered invaluable aid to the wounded.[11]

As the fire raged, Kyle's radio operator contributed to the chaos. This well-meaning but misguided airman took it upon himself to broadcast in the blind that the two aircraft had collided. Unfortunately, the excited operator omitted his call

Side view of a special operations C-130 aircraft in flight. The Air Force used six C-130s at Desert One. Two carried fuel for the helicopters and departed the site before the collision took place. (U.S. Air Force)

This large, stained glass window, a memorial to the eight men who died at Desert One, was installed in the Hurlburt Air Force Chapel, Fort Walton Beach, Florida, on 23 April 1982. The eight who gave their lives were: Captain Lyn D. McIntosh, Captain Richard L. Bakke, Captain Harold L. Lewis, Jr., Captain Charles T. McMillan, and Technical Sergeant Joel C. Mayo, all of the air force. Staff Sergeant Dewey L. Johnson, Sergeant John D. Harvey, and Corporal George N. Holmes were marines. (U.S. Air Force)

sign in the message, so that the originator was unknown to the tense radiomen listening on board the *Nimitz* and at General Vaught's command post. Repeated radio queries failed to reveal the identity of the sender. It is likely that with so many simultaneous transmissions being sent on the same frequency, each operator blocked out the other.

Back in Washington, General Jones finally received news of the crash at 5:15 P.M. and telephoned the sad news to the White House. Only at 11:00 P.M. did the president learn that eight service men had lost their lives. Allegedly, a civilian agent also was killed. Undoubtedly, he was an Iranian interpreter.[12]

A Ticklish Takeoff

As exploding fuel tanks and ammunition lighted up the sky, a fusillade of debris sprayed three helicopters, parked within fifty yards of the devouring flames. With his men in immediate peril from the explosions, Kyle gave the order to evacuate the site as quickly as possible and not to take time to destroy the helicopters. Marines and soldiers, responding quickly, boarded the three remaining transport planes. All the while, C-130 crews frantically jettisoned motorcycles, jeeps, and weapons in order to provide seating space. Thirty minutes after the explosion, the air force pilots loaded the survivors on board, taxied into position, and flew out without further incident. The aircraft had been on the ground for over four hours.[13]

Colonel Beckwith described his departure as "a real unique takeoff." Asked to explain, he described how his plane, in picking up flying speed, ran across a three-feet-high embankment, bounced down, and then took off. All aircraft headed for Masirah, where they landed. The wounded, among whom was the severely burned Major Schaefer, were met by a C-141 "medevac" plane waiting to transport them to Egypt, where a medical unit skilled in burn treatment was on hand to treat them. All nonwounded boarded a C-141 and were flown to Egypt and thence home to North Carolina.[14]

The evidence shows that, despite the carnage, the marines were prepared to destroy their helicopters and secret materials. In fact, two of the helicopter crews removed classified documents. The pilot of helo 4, a marine captain who asked that his name not be mentioned, revealed to a newspaper reporter that the helicopter crew was told by "the boss" (Lieutenant Colonel Seiffert) to "get out of the bird and prepare to destruct." This order was countermanded by Kyle's decision to abandon the helos forthwith. The Holloway review board found that there was no evidence that Kyle was aware that classified material was being left behind.

If his men had returned to salvage material from three

Four Swiss policemen stand guard over the coffins of the Americans killed in Iran. In the group of officials in the center is Archbishop Hilarion Capudji who accompanied the coffins to Zurich, where they were given to the International Red Cross, which in turn passed them on to American authorities. (AP–Wirephoto)

helicopters near the blazing fire, their attempt might have cost lives, delayed departure, and even risked damage to the C-130s from random explosions. But the fact remains that military men are expected to protect secret documents with their lives, if necessary. More than twenty minutes remained before the C-130s took off. Probably because of security, Colonel Kyle was uninformed of the classified papers in the helos and, consequently, ordered the helo crews to board the C-130s immediately.

In his subsequent report of the mission, General Jones, chairman of the Joint Chiefs of Staff, announced that in the judgment of Colonel Kyle, explosive destruction of the helicopters would have made an already dangerous situation unmanageable, and it would have greatly jeopardized the C-130s and many lives. As a result, Khomeini's men recovered the material, permitting the Iranian press and television to carry photos of captured maps as evidence of Washington's "satanic" plan.

The heat, flames, and explosions must have hastened Kyle's decision, but the Holloway panel administered a rebuke in its comments on the capture of secret material by the Iranians: "The loss of classified material . . . reflects unfavorably on the performance of the personnel involved. Their actions resulted in possible enemy exploitation of sensitive material, including its use for propaganda ends." This low-key admonishment most probably had reference to maps showing safe houses for secret agents; lists of radio call signs and frequencies; and photographs of locations, such as a warehouse used to hide the trucks destined to bring the commandos from Desert Two to the embassy compound.

Kyle, whose main task was to command the C-130s, seemingly was as ignorant of the presence of secret documents in the helos as the helicopter crews may have been of the identity of their on-site commander. Such were the handicaps imposed by too stringent secrecy.[15]

Although there is no indication that Khomeini's soldiers ever captured U.S. agents in Tehran, the breach of security at

Desert One surely endangered their lives. Beckwith recounts that the command center at Qena signaled the agents that the mission had been canceled. He also recalls that either he or Colonel Kyle said, "Let's get an air strike in on them (the five helicopters)." Kyle conveyed this suggestion to General Vaught and requested authority to call in the attack aircraft. His recommendation was not accepted. Reportedly Carter rejected the idea in order not to jeopardize the forty-five Iranian bus riders left at Desert One. Later Beckwith regretted that he had not had an M16 loaded with tracers to "set those damned machines afire."

As reported in *Time*, President Carter called for a copy of President Kennedy's televised explanation following the Bay of Pigs calamity. After several hours of sleep, he arose to draft a statement to the American people.[16]

6

A Worldwide Flareup

Uproar in Washington

On 25 April 1980, an anguished President Carter, seated at his desk before the television crews, announced that he had recalled a carefully planned mission to rescue the hostages, which had failed because of mechanical difficulties. He praised the brave men who had died, accepted the responsibility for the tragedy, and promised to pursue every avenue for the release of the hostages by peaceful means. That same day all U.S. embassies were authorized to release a statement that emphasized that the president himself had canceled the mission and that equipment failure was the prime cause.

On the next day, when the White House had learned the full extent of the disaster, Carter, in letters to Senator Robert Byrd and House Speaker T. P. "Tip" O'Neill, gave more details. Possibly with an eye to placating congressional leaders, who, for security reasons, had not been kept fully informed, Carter explained that he had carried out the operation under the authority of the War Powers Resolution section 8(d)(1) and the United Nations Charter, Article 51, relating to the protection of citizens in a foreign land. He disclosed that "the rescue team was under my overall command and control and required my approval before executing the subsequent phases of the operation." While this presidential assumption of command was commendable, it did not absolve the military of any blame that might ensue. Presidents cannot, nor are they expected to, exercise command and control of a combat operation thousands of miles away.[1]

Former CIA director and former secretary of defense James R. Schlesinger, who had served under Presidents Nixon and Ford, commended Carter as courageous but condemned the mission as too complex. In an indirect jab at the Pentagon, he asserted that the decision to carry out the raid unfortunately revealed that the high command, in its desire to demonstrate combat capability, had allowed its "can-do" zeal to override prudence. As if in rebuttal to such a charge, General Jones had disclosed at a Pentagon press conference several days before that when the idea of the rescue was originally broached, the Chiefs had considered it infeasible. As the planning continued, however, they decided that the problems, which had initially been viewed as insurmountable, were solvable. The Chiefs thus maintained that they had agreed to the presidential proposal only after a long, hard look.[2]

Investigative action was not long in coming. A few days after the president's television appearance, the Senate Armed Services Committee began closed hearings, specifically on helicopter upkeep, equipment performance, and support facilities. Senate Majority Leader Robert C. Byrd had pressed for an inquiry, his particular concerns being helicopter malfunctioning, aircraft maintenance, and technical training.[3]

The new "get-tough" mood on Captiol Hill suggested that the nation had cast off its post-Vietnam aversion to all things military. The failure of three out of eight helicopters was a clear signal to many in Congress of inadequate readiness.

Editorials criticized past cheeseparing of defense policies that had shrunk the fighting forces. Voters wondered how a nation so advanced technologically could have botched the raid so badly. Some questioned whether a military rescue was really necessary. And, at any rate, why was the operation run in such a way that command cohesion seemed singularly weak? Others cautioned that the disaster should not be blown out of proportion, that it was a onetime episode from which valuable military lessons might be learned.

Stung by allegations that the eight Navy helicopters may not have been in top condition, Admiral Thomas Hayward, the chief of naval operations (CNO), hastened to set the record straight. In a little noticed public speech, he replied to those civilian experts who had "let loose a crescendo of uninformed recrimination" in their thirst for scapegoats. Demanding that critics stop blaming the combat men in the operation, he declared that it was the Joint Chiefs who had "let America down."

Hayward went further: If the president "was led down the wrong path," the blame resided with the JCS. Vaught's men should not be castigated for lack of professional competence or ability; they did all they were asked to do and more, said the CNO. His spirited defense was well received but did nothing to explain the Joint Chiefs' estimate that the raid had a good chance of success. The Chiefs seem to have failed to examine past covert operations—a serious, avoidable mistake. The record, historically, leans heavily toward failure, not success. According to a U.S. Air Force expert, 75 percent of the World War II commando raids executed by British intelligence and the Office of Special Services failed. Moreover, an analysis of Vietnam operations shows that U.S. forces attempted ninety-one POW rescue missions but that only twenty were successful. Perhaps these missions were justified in spite of the high costs. The point is that, statistically, covert operations are high-risk gambles, a fact that the White House and the Pentagon may not have sufficiently appreciated.[4]

Criticism in the Press

When the American people learned the full extent of the calamity, the majority agreed with the president that the rescue was the right action at the time. Traditionally, in time of national crisis, Americans rally around the president. Nevertheless, favorable public opinion polls were not sufficient to quell press criticism on why the operation had misfired.

Newsweek raised several questions: Were the helicopters sufficiently tested for a six-hundred-mile flight at low altitudes in poor visibility? Was the plan too elaborate and fragile? How could the raiders assault the embassy without creating heavy casualties? Should the raid have been attempted at all? *Business Week* found the Pentagon and Jimmy Carter wanting in good judgment by expecting too much of complex aircraft that were prone to failure. The high command had traded reliability for performance by placing too much faith in complicated war machines, said the editorial writer.[5]

The *National Review*, rarely an admirer of the president, scored the administration for using fourteen-year-old helicopters (this was untrue; the aircraft averaged seven years of service, not an excessive time) that had been shipped to Diego Garcia and reassembled there. The article correctly pointed out, however, that the loss of eight helicopters had stripped the Navy of one-third of its helicopter aerial minesweeping force.[6]

Time awarded the administration an A for effort, an F for executive competence, and asked if Carter had mounted a rescue because of the presidential race. Other critics condemned the tentativeness of the aborted raid, pointing out that shaving the margin of safety (to eight helos) betrayed a lack of conviction. Others charged that the plan was too lean and lacked enough men and aircraft to carry out the mission.[7]

A few experts dealt harshly with the chain of command that had placed the task force commander back in Egypt and linked by instant communication to the White House and the Pentagon, as well as to Colonels Kyle and Beckwith at Desert One. Such a tenuous setup not only violated unity of command, it contained seeds of destruction when combat contingencies left no time to consult, said Edward Luttwak, a defense specialist at Georgetown University. For success in special operations, Luttwak prescribed certain rules: avoid all technical risks; do not rely on too few inherently fragile aircraft; have decisive superiority at the point of contact. Measured against these rules, critics believed that the rescue plan failed on two out of three counts, if one concedes that Beckwith would have had a superior force at the embassy.[8]

Barbs from Foreign Capitals

From abroad, foreign spokesmen joined in the chorus of censure. The opinion in Europe, as sampled by *Time*, was that Carter was not up to leading the United States or its allies. *U.S. News & World Report* described foreign disdain of the United States's incompetence, naiveté, and false sense of priorities. London's *New Statesman* argued that if the assault force had reached Tehran, many would have died and the lives of Americans working in Iran would have been jeopardized. The entire event had only strengthened the hands of the Islamic fundamentalists, according to this commentator.

Carter's decision to keep European leaders in the dark on the raid caused bitterness and disappointment, reported *Business Week*. The rescue attempt came only three days after West European nations and Japan had announced their intention to enforce sanctions against Iran, agreeing to these steps apparently on the assumption that President Carter would not resort to military measures. NATO's secretary general, Dr. Joseph Luns of the Netherlands, denounced the raid as further complicating the delicate situation in Tehran. Allied governments supported Luns and warned against any second rescue attempt. Nonetheless, for humanitarian reasons and in spite of their resentment, the allies agreed to sustain diplomatic and economic sanctions against Iran, while the fate of the hostages remained in doubt.[9]

In Moscow the failed rescue provided ammunition for Tass, the Soviet news agency. Smarting from world criticism in the wake of the Christmas-day invasion of Afghanistan, the Kremlin leadership instructed the propagandists to condemn the rescue operation as an aberration "bordering on the brink of madness" and a "serious danger to world peace and security." Tass doubted that any member of NATO could accept anyone as an ally who was as "dictatorial and reckless" as Carter. Could NATO hope that he would consult them in the event he considered using U.S. missiles deployed in Europe, asked Tass. The answer, presumably, was self-evident.[10]

A Second Rescue Attempt?

News of the action at Desert One was slow in filtering through to Tehran. Not until 11 P.M. on 25 April did word reach the guards at the embassy compound. Hurriedly ordering the prisoners to pack, the Iranians herded them into vans. Within twenty-four hours, the captives were dispersed to remote hiding places miles from Tehran. It was not until six weeks later that the captives learned of the operation and, then, only in bits and pieces. One captive, surprisingly, was informed in a letter from an American child who expressed sorrow that the rescue had failed. Would there be another attempt?[11]

The collapse of the operation did not shut off further plans to free the hostages. But because of the coming of short summer nights and the insufficient hours of darkness, the chances of a future raid were unlikely. Additionally, having once alarmed the Iranians, U.S. forces could no longer count on the element of surprise.

Yet in the Carter White House, hope for another rescue continued to stir. Two days after the task force's return from Desert One, Brzezinski, in response to Carter's order, began organizing a second assault. He does not name his associates, but states that "we decided" on a larger force of commandos to be transported directly to Tehran. We do not know if Carter abandoned the idea of a naval blockade on Iran's coast or the mining of Persian Gulf maritime choke points. But we have learned that members of the task force were kept in training for some time for what they called the "second half of the ball game." It is likely that the White House finally sensed that under the circumstances, the administration should rely more

on negotiations rather than force. Carter subsequently believed that the Desert One debacle marked a turning point in
his try for reelection. It also ended, although he did not know
it at the time, any hope that he, as president, could welcome
home the prisoners on their release by Khomeini.[12]

Secretary Brown and General Jones Meet the Press

The day following the raid, 25 April 1980, Defense Secretary
Brown met with the press in the Pentagon. In his summary of
events leading up to Desert One, Brown emphasized that
although the mission had been complex and difficult, in his
judgment and that of the Joint Chiefs, it was operationally
feasible. The mission, he said, was the best course of "getting
our hostages out of Iran expeditiously" with the "least risk of
harming the Iranian people." He then answered questions on
operational details.

In one response Brown declared that the operation was
not an attack on Iran in any way. Immediately a reporter
asked, "How come you don't see that tensions would not have
arisen if you didn't confront and probably kill a few Iranians?"
Dismissing the question because it was "not fruitful to specu-
late," Brown added that "a successful rescue would have
affected them [Iran] favorably." He avoided any discussion on
how the Delta force could have rescued the hostages without
considerable casualties.[13]

A journalist asked if the aborted rescue ruled out "any
further American military effort." Brown replied that "we"
(the administration) were not going to rule out any option.
But he continued to believe that a peaceful solution was the
best solution.

A reporter, mystified by the assumption that the mission
was humanitarian in nature, addressed Brown:

> Question: Mr. Secretary, how could you have secured the
> release of the hostages without massive blood-
> shed, given the fact that there is (sic) an esti-
> mated 150 armed Iranian militants guarding the
> Embassy?

Brown: I am not going into the details of any parts of the mission, beyond the parts that were actually carried out. I will say that the Joint Chiefs of Staff reviewed this; I reviewed it; and the team itself was convinced that that was the part of the mission of which they were most confident.

Brown came off rather well in the exchange, save for his refusal to explain how the spilling of blood could have been avoided. Certainly Colonel Beckwith fully expected that the Iranian guards would be, as he later phrased it, "blown away."[14]

At a second news conference on 29 April, Brown fielded more questions. He made clear that when the Joint Chiefs had declared the operation to be militarily feasible, they spoke from a military point of view. He added that the operation was not a military one but a rescue, a term with a different connotation. Finally Brown asserted that he had considered other factors as well, such as the consequence of failure in terms of international politics and alternative diplomatic actions. What these consequences might have been he did not explain. In the meantime, President Carter directed the Pentagon to bring a reluctant Colonel Beckwith to Washington to face the press, because, Beckwith wrote, there were reports that the president and Beckwith "were at an impasse over the wisdom of conducting the mission." It was Beckwith's task to dispel this rumor.[15]

Beckwith's Pentagon News Conference

Nine days after the raid, on 1 May 1980, the unwilling colonel, dressed in a civilian suit, met with media reporters in the Pentagon pressroom. All photographers were banned, presumably in an effort to prevent revenge-seeking terrorists from recognizing him from news photos. A Defense Department press officer stated that the meeting was called so that Beckwith could quell rumors that he had opposed the order to abort and would have pressed on with five helicopters if the decision had been his to make.[16]

Facing the national press corps, Beckwith came through as a tough, professional fighter unskilled in the folkways of Washington. He yes-ma'amed and yes-sirred the reporters, but his blunt replies lacked the finesse normally expected of a senior officer.

Question: Colonel, there are rumors that you are going to retire or resign in protest [or] something of that sort?

Beckwith: That's [expletive], sir.

Question: Did you have a point of no return like if those [helicopters] weren't ready to fly out by hour X, no go?

Beckwith: There was a point of [no] return but I would appreciate it if you wouldn't quote me on it because that was the air part of it [a responsibility of Colonel Kyle] and I wasn't read into it. I was the ground task force.

Question: What I meant is on the ground. In other words you as the field commander—didn't have your six helicopters by the certain hour and you said, well, there is not enough light left so we scrub [cancel].

Beckwith: And we would abort, sir.

Question: Was there a time on the ground [beyond which the task force could not remain]?

Beckwith: Yes. Yes, there was . . . I am already an hour late [on the mission schedule].

Question: Did you have some colorful words for those choppers [helicopters] being late?

Beckwith: Yes, sir.

Question: Did you give them a little hell for being late?

Beckwith: Ah—if I did, I don't mean to. I usually give a lot of people hell, sir. My soldiers are on time and I expect all other people to try to get on time, sir. I try to be punctual—I don't appreciate it. I had no idea and it wasn't until yesterday, in fact, that I realized the ordeal the helicopter pilots had experienced.

Beckwith flared at a reporter who suggested that he was disposed to go ahead with five helos but was overruled. "With all due respect, sir," he said, "you don't know where you're coming from. I am not about to be a party to a [expletive] loading of a bunch of aircraft and going up and murdering a bunch of the finest soldiers in the world. I wouldn't do that. It burns me up because I'm not that type of man." He emphasized that he alone recommended to Colonel Kyle to abort; that the radio messages to General Vaught were to inform his superiors and not for their permission to abandon the mission. The interview continued:

> Question: Would you recall your decision moment again? Was it quickly that you . . .
>
> Beckwith: That was the easiest decision to make, sir. We rehearsed this. I didn't make the decision, but the recommendation I made was very easy.
>
> Question: Could you tell us what went through your mind?
>
> Beckwith: I said, my God, I am going to fail . . . The only thing I had on my mind was we failed and I have got to get out of here . . . The watch was ticking. I was getting worried about being caught somewhere in the desert of Iran at first light.

With regard to allegations that the operations plan was unsound, Beckwith affirmed that it was "fine," and he would not have changed anything, "not me." When asked if certain equipment and men had been denied him, he replied, "Nothing was denied. We used conventional equipment."

A short time later Beckwith was transferred from the Delta team to a staff billet at the Joint Special Operations Command at Fort Bragg, North Carolina. True to type, he denigrated the assignment because "it ain't as good a job [as leading a combat team], I'll tell you that. It's a goddam paper job." He went on to add, "Yeah, I'm old-fashioned patriotic. I believe in the flag, apple pie, and John Wayne." In this offhand remark, said half in jest, Beckwith perhaps spoke with more truth than he knew.

The Return of the Hostages

On 20 January 1981, only two minutes after President Ronald Reagan had taken the oath of office, Khomeini released the fifty-two hostages (Richard Queen, a Foreign Service Officer, had been released by Khomeini on 11 July 1980 after 250 days in captivity because of an illness later diagnosed as multiple sclerosis). Apparently, the vengeful mullah intended the odd timing as a final humiliation of his arch enemy, Carter. Others attributed the early release to reports that if the hostages were not delivered forthwith, Reagan would stop all negotiations and, without warning, take direct action that would end any chance of Iran's recovery of billions of dollars held by Washington.

The release was arranged by the government of Algeria, which acted as mediator during the closing days of Carter's term. The resourceful, diligent Algerians negotiated an agreement calling for the prisoners to be freed in exchange for the transfer by the United States of some $8 billion in escrow accounts to the Bank of England. Of this amount, $2.8 billion went directly to Iran. Several more billions were paid to U.S. bank claimants. Another $2 billion was placed in the custody of the Central Bank of the Netherlands to await judgment by a claims tribunal at the Hague. The financial holdings of the Shah's family were not a factor in the negotiations.[17]

According to *Time* magazine, Carter believed that if the mission had succeeded, his reelection would have been assured. Such reasoning supports the truism that an official in public life tends to evaluate a crisis in terms of how his performance will influence his political future and, ultimately, his place in history. For all Carter's professed desire to prevent what he saw as the imminent murder of the Americans, he and his staff were not blind to the political benefits that would flow from a bold, dramatic raid. The other side of the coin, which he may not have considered, was the probability that if the raid failed, he would be turned out of office, partly because of the public's frustration with the low state of U.S. prestige in the wake of the aborted rescue.

7

The Holloway Investigation

A Limited Inquiry

Like other national disasters, the Iranian rescue attempt demanded an inquiry. In such episodes, certain aspects are apt to be kept under wraps; in matters of state, nations are reluctant to reveal their secrets to their adversaries through boards of investigation. For all that, outcries in the press and in the Congress persuaded the administration to disclose some answers on why the raid had been bungled. To avoid a formal congressional investigation, the administration arranged for the appointment of a military review group. In the Pentagon, the story went the rounds that White House spokesmen had requested congressional leaders to delay any formal probe until the military professionals had assembled the facts.

The term *review group*, uncommon in military law, avoided the negative connotations associated with military courts. For example, calamities, accidents, and mishaps generally are examined by boards of investigation, courts of inquiry, or simple one-officer investigations. The six-officer review group, appointed by General Jones, was instructed to delve only into the military causes of the failure—what went

wrong and why—and to identify the military lessons learned
and how the services could apply them in the future. Con-
versely, its instructions were to avoid identifying any individual whom they might judge to be negligent or culpable in
planning or executing the mission.

Admiral James L. Holloway III headed the
review group, which was charged with identifying the military lessons learned from the
aborted rescue mission so that the services
could apply them in future planning. (U.S.
Navy)

In contrast with formal investigations, the review group was limited in its authority. For example, a court of inquiry can name "interested parties" and take testimony from witnesses, who are allowed counsel and the privilege of cross-examination. A board of investigation can establish the facts, hear testimony, and make findings. A board of investigation and court of inquiry can recommend further legal action, as can a single officer appointed to conduct a simple investigation. The Holloway review group had no such authority. Its sole purpose was to ascertain those operational and matériel deficiencies in need of modification for future operations. Its conclusions were to be forwarded to General Jones. In compliance with its charter, the panel, in its sanitized report, made no mention of the president, the White House, the defense secretary, or the Joint Chiefs of Staff. The classified version of the report, as of 1984, had not been released.[1]

Holloway's Team of Experts

Admiral Holloway and his colleagues, as longtime career officers, probably accepted their appointment as a matter of duty but with little enthusiasm. Ordinarily, people take no satisfaction in sitting in judgment on individuals who have been handed a difficult and dangerous assignment and failed. Holloway, then fifty-eight years old and a veteran of thirty-seven years of naval service, had been named by the JCS to act as chairman. The son of an admiral and a graduate of the U.S. Naval Academy class of 1943, he had retired in 1978 from the post of chief of naval operations. His background was that of a fighter pilot, carrier skipper, commander of the Seventh Fleet in the Far East, and member of the Joint Chiefs of Staff. Professionally able, quick-witted, and articulate, he had succeeded in raising the combat standards of the service while fending off budget cutters who had brought the navy down to 470 ships.

The other five members, all generals in the army, air force, or Marine Corps, merit brief description. All were experienced in clandestine or special operations, but none had been involved in the Tehran rescue mission or had any previous knowledge of it before 25 April 1980. Three of the generals were retired, and two were in active service.[2]

Retired army Lieutenant General Samuel V. Wilson, fifty-seven, was an expert in counterinsurgency, guerrilla warfare, and intelligence operations. Air force Lieutenant General Leroy J. Manor, fifty-nine, also a retired officer, was a former commander of the air force special operations force. In 1970 he had been the commander of the joint task force for the SonTay operation in North Vietnam. Although no American POWs were rescued (they had been transferred to another site), the SonTay operation was so technically well executed that, some said, it had served as a model for the Israeli rescue at Entebbe.

Major General James C. Smith, fifty-seven, had been the army's director of training. As a helicopter pilot, he had done important work in developing the army air units in the Korean and Vietnam wars. Air force Major General John L. Piotrowski, forty-six, currently was deputy commander for air defense in the Tactical Air Command. A pilot and an electronics warfare specialist, he was known for his work in commando operations as well as for his knowledge of airborne warning and control procedures. The sixth member of the group, Major General Alfred M. Gray, fifty-two, of the Marine Corps, was the deputy director of the Development Center at Quantico, Virginia. A combat veteran with long experience in unconventional warfare, he was an expert in joint operations and electronic intelligence and countermeasures.

A High-Risk Gamble

Although these six officers from four services initially believed that consensus would be difficult, they discovered to their surprise that they were unanimous in their findings. Some two years after the investigation, Admiral Holloway recalled that, at the start, all members acknowledged privately that the mission had been "very poorly handled [planned] and very poorly executed." But at the end of the inquiry, each member had changed his opinion to one of the "greatest admiration for the people who planned and tried to execute the most difficult operation you could possibly have undertaken." This admiration, mingled with muted criticism, comes through clearly in the report.

Holloway also emphasized that incredible misfortune dogged the operation. "You had to have an operation involving forces small enough to get to the wall of the Embassy undetected, yet big enough and tough enough to fight your way out of Iran. So that was a hell of a problem. I really think that [the JCS, Vaught and his staff] had the only possible solution. I think [the mission] had a 60 to 70% chance of success and ran into some terribly bad luck."[3]

On the other hand, the investigators found that the rescue effort was by its very nature a high-risk proposition with real possibilities of failure. People and equipment were to be called upon to perform at extreme limits of ability where there was little margin to compensate for mistakes or ill fortune. They also agreed that the idea of a small, clandestine assault, although hazardous, was valid and that as a military operation it was "consistent with [that is, supported] national policy objectives." In brief, as the report states, "it offered the best chance of getting out the hostages alive and the least danger of starting a war with Iran." This latter statement, one may assume, represented an evaluation by the JCS, who had been tasked by the White House to produce a rescue plan.

Although the members found planning deficiencies, they concluded that "no one action or lack of action caused the operation to fail, and that no one alternative or all the alternatives [measures suggested by the Holloway group] could have guaranteed its success." We are left with the impression that the panel believed that the task force had been handed an extremely high-risk mission, that the high risk was manageable, and that bad luck had doomed the operation, which had little margin for the unexpected.[4]

It may be true that bad luck was a factor in the debacle. If fortune had favored Vaught's men, they would have brought back the hostages, and President Carter might have fared better in his political career. In a somewhat similar situation, one could surmise that the British expedition to the Falklands in 1982 was a success because of the bad luck of the Argentine air force in failing to sink more ships. If its planes and missiles had sunk one of the two enemy carriers, the British task force and Mrs. Thatcher's political future may well have faced disaster. Instead, the Royal Navy's air and naval power prevailed, the Falklands were retaken, and Margaret Thatcher's reelection was assured. In short, one person's bad luck will be his adversary's unexpected good luck. In military operations, as in everyday life, mishaps are more likely if the risk is high.

Collecting the Evidence

In their search for evidence, Holloway and his panel reviewed all documents relating to the planning, training, logistics, post mission debriefings, congressional hearings, media reports, press releases, helicopter performance analyses, and the official after-action report. They traveled to all field facilities involved in the mission, and although no bases are named, it is likely that the areas near Nellis Air Force Base, forty miles from Las Vegas, Nevada; the Marine Corps Air Station and the Army Proving Ground, both at Yuma, Arizona; and Fort Bragg, North Carolina (home of the Army Special Forces), were all on the itinerary.

At the various training sites, the panel examined equipment and received briefings by officers and civilian technical experts on every aspect of the operation. They inspected helicopters, checked C-130s specially configured for secret operations, and flew mock combat missions in helicopters fitted with special equipment. And they witnessed a demonstration by an army team simulating the recovery of hostages from a terrorist-held building and a hijacked aircraft.

The panel members were equally thorough in their interviews with the military, but the report does not state whether they met with President Carter, Dr. Brzezinski, or senior civilian officials. The group, after all, was limited to a military inquiry. To underline this fact, the panel declared that the majority of discussions were with the military and that the investigation was confined to organizations and procedures within the national military command system. This latter statement could mean that the panel met with President Carter, as commander in chief, and with his deputy, Secretary of Defense Brown. One also could assume the panel had a legitimate interest in talking to Dr. Brzezinski concerning his role in the operation. In any event, the report makes clear that every person whom the panel desired to interview "was made available."

To gain a close-up view of the combatants, their particular combat skills, and even their unit morale, panel members sat in round-table discussions with all ranks and grades. These sessions, according to the report, provided "useful insights," an expression that may be interpreted to mean that the Holloway group learned the unvarnished truth of any deficiencies from General Vaught and his men.[5]

Guidelines for the Inquiry

Limited to tactical and technical matters, the panel devised a simple procedure. After reading all the evidence, listening to all witnesses, and inspecting operational units, each member wrote down a list of items that "troubled" him. The panel then categorized these items into areas of concern and further refined them into specific issues. Individual members then analyzed each issue, first in terms of the facts and, second, in terms of the rationale of General Vaught and his staff. Finally, they evaluated the net impact of each issue on the mission and the degree to which it had affected the outcome.

The panel next developed alternative "solutions" to each issue and tested them to see whether they would have achieved the goal and at what cost. Those alternative solutions that "failed" the test as impractical or clearly inferior were eliminated along with the issue. In these cases, then, the panel concurred with the course of action actually taken. The group also determined whether the alternative solution would have improved the overall chances for success. In its deliberations, the panel tried to reach a consensus on each issue. If unable to agree, a member was authorized to set down his separate view as a footnote or a dissent. As noted, the panel members were unanimous in their conclusions.

In writing its report, the panel made no attempt to duplicate the secret, after-action report prepared for the JCS by General Vaught and his subcommanders. The investigators did, however, examine the soundness and suitability of the plan (its "conceptual validity," in General Jones's words) and its feasibility. The members also pondered the planning process, including the veil of secrecy that hung over the entire plan. Last, they considered the effect of any "guidance" that may have been given General Vaught by the White House or his Pentagon superiors.

By the end of the inquiry, the panel had identified twenty-three issues that suggested errors of judgment or required remedial action, some of which we discuss below.[6]

An Initial Organizational Error

As we know, General Vaught at the outset chose to ignore the Joint Chiefs' relevant contingency plan and its crisis response procedure and, instead, laboriously built up an untried organization with a new command-and-control system. He may have reasoned that if he had used the readily available JCS system, the security risk might have been greater simply because more Joint Staff officers would have been involved. The Holloway panel did not agree, pointing out that if appropriate security precautions had been observed, General Vaught would have had excellent prospects that security would have remained tight, the planning preparation phase accelerated, and overall readiness improved. The inference is clear: Vaught had erred.[7]

The JCS contingency plan for emergencies in Iran contained a wide range of options for the use of military force in the Middle East. True, the JCS did not have a plan specifically tailored for an assault on the embassy compound, but Vaught would have had a framework on which to build. In short, the mission planners would have enjoyed a running start in mounting the rescue, yet Vaught chose to organize the task force from scratch. So he was forced to make liberal use of specially created methods, a procedure that met with frowns from the investigators, who noted that "prolonged ad hoc arrangements often result in tasking from different sources and can cause confusion at the operating level."

Put another way, General Vaught could have improved his command framework by using the Joint Chiefs' emergency crisis action system (CAS). He then could have alerted and received instant support from the commanders in chief of the unified commands in the Atlantic, Pacific, and Europe and the commanders of the Strategic Air Command and the Rapid Deployment Force. Furthermore, if intelligence functions had been assigned to the DIA director, this officer could have demanded and obtained efficient support from all intelligence agencies.[8]

Throughout the Holloway analysis, there runs the thought that operational security was enforced too zealously. We do not know if General Vaught ever protested to General Jones that compartmentation was injuring his operation, for the Holloway report is silent on the point. Possibly aware that some might interpret their criticism as an indictment of "able and brave men," Holloway, speaking for the panel, assured his readers that not a shred of evidence of culpable neglect or incompetence was found. The group, in fact, concluded that the risks were manageable, the chances of success were good, and the decision justified.[9]

The Holloway report was even more critical of Vaught's communication procedures. The basic JCS contingency plan contained tested methods and command procedures for communication, which, in previous secret operations, had proved that operational security could be preserved. Further, if Vaught had employed *selective*, rather than *minimum*, disclosure to individuals, he would have had stronger unity of command and task force cohesion, as well as better command

and control and overall readiness. Decisions regarding security should have aimed at a balance between compartmentation on the one hand and, on the other, sound organization, planning, and preparation. The conclusion seems inescapable that whoever had insisted that security be the dominant factor in mission planning and execution had committed a grave and costly error.[10]

Training by Remote Control

Because of terrain requirements and logistics demands, the task force used training sites scattered throughout the United States, and General Vaught's difficulties in personally supervising these distant bases were magnified because he did not name a deputy commander for training. This supervision by remote control was not the way a general officer normally would have carried out such an assignment. Traditionally, senior officers in Vaught's position would have delegated authority for joint training to a qualified officer.

When Vaught decided to direct all training from his Pentagon office, he assumed formidable tasks, including overview of training schedules, operational support to the bases, administrative assistance in matters such as personnel, and aid from outside agencies (as for example, more helicopters from the Navy). For on-site conferences and inspections, his staff officers commuted by air to the training sites. Critiques of training were sent from the field to Washington by secure telephone, by teletype, or by personal reports by returning staff officers. In some instances, the general himself was present at exercises.

One positive feature of General Vaught's supervision were the conferences conducted after each training exercise, which proved very effective in uncovering problems in procedures and equipment and suggesting remedial action. But training exercises suffered in that pilots and crews of the C-130s and helicopters were not briefed in a body before every joint exercise on the Nevada desert. Nor were they "critiqued" (evaluated) jointly after every drill. In some cases,

after an exercise, C-130 crews flew back to their home base
without a face-to-face exchange of information with helicopter pilots and Army Rangers and Green Berets. Failure to
conduct immediate critiques made impossible an oral exchange of views, which, in turn, would have reduced confusion and cleared up misunderstandings. Taking note of these
oversights, the panel bluntly said that "the combat readiness
of the task force would have been improved." This can be read
to mean that the force was not up to the highest standards.[11]

To give added punch to its findings, the panel recommended that in any similar operation, the Joint Chiefs set up a
centralized training site separated from task force headquarters. One can take this as a hint that Vaught's staff officers or
some individuals in Washington made decisions (or failed to
do so) on training matters, which the subcommanders, who
were the actual combatants, did not always find acceptable.

What would have been the benefits if Vaught had named
a deputy commander with a small staff to supervise coordinated training? This deputy would have arranged for joint
mission briefings, critiques, and periodic progress reports. As
a general officer, this deputy could have moved fast to correct
shortcomings; allocate funds, supplies, and aircraft for the
training components; and, in the panel's words, "contributed
positively to morale." This last phrase points unmistakably to
the frustrations of subcommanders, far from Washington,
attempting to "get some action" on their requests for aid. That
is, a deputy in charge of the training program would have
improved its precision, speed of execution, and interunit coordination. Furthermore, problem areas in the operation would
have been uncovered (particularly in communications) and
necessary changes made.[12]

The Penalties of an Informal Command Structure

The panel found that "command-and-control [the authority
to specify not only *what* is to be done but *how*, including
planning, directing, and controlling of an operation] was excellent at the upper echelons but tenuous and fragile at in-

termediate levels." Mid-level command relationships were
not always clearly defined or emphasized. In some cases they
were even misunderstood or misinterpreted; at Desert One
marine pilots questioned orders to abandon their helicopters
because they did not even know that air force Colonel Kyle
was the site commander.

As isolated detachments continued to rehearse their respective roles in the plan, they had little or no knowledge of
other units. The Holloway report noted sharply that General
Vaught (not named but identifiable) planned and conducted
training "within an informal command structure that does not
appear to have been clearly established."[13]

The panel pinpointed other weaknesses. Isolated detachment commanders at remote sites, early on, had realized that
they needed on-site support for delivery of spare parts, new
communication equipment, replacement aircraft, and the like.
They later testified that they had encountered difficulties in
obtaining such support and administrative help. A likely cause
for any inadequate support was an overcentralized command
center and an overloaded staff. On the plus side, the investigators singled out for commendation the system that secretly
supplied spare parts for the navy's helicopters, especially in
light of the problems imposed by operational security.[14]

Vaught's problems were also made more difficult by
occasional White House alerts that the rescue force be prepared
to take off for Iran on very short notice. The Holloway report
revealed as much: "The dynamic situation [including negotiations with Iran] required some mission capability [that is, the
task force must be ready to go any time] from mid December
1979 to 24 April 1980." The doughty Beckwith confirmed this
on-again, off-again state of affairs. In a television interview
two years after the raid, Beckwith recalled:

> I was told about seven times to get ready to go [on the
> assault] and you put the sharp edge on your personnel and
> then you tell them to stand down and it has an impact. So I
> would say after the seventh time, "If we're going to do this
> particular event, we need to *do* it because I can get my

troops up one more time; and the ninth time, I'm not so sure, because they've been like a yo-yo—they've been up and they've been down."[15]

Obviously in Beckwith's view, his superiors had put his group on the alert so many times that training requirements were never stabilized.

Why was the command chain faulty? The answer was that while there was a clear line of authority from the president to the defense secretary and the chairman of the Joint Chiefs of Staff, the task force command channels were "less well defined in some areas and only implied in others." In other words, Holloway and his colleagues emphasized the absence of a clear-cut chain of command with tightly defined responsibilities, but it is not apparent in the report why this condition was not corrected in time. It is clear, however, that the fuzzy line of command, coupled with the absence of completely integrated training, meant that the task force never achieved its full potential.[16]

No Full Dress Rehearsal

Under pressure to expedite training and at the same time maintain the primacy of security, Vaught decided that "regular integration of training [units] was undesirable." In other words, the troops, the C-130s, and the helicopters never conducted a joint, full dress rehearsal, with all elements participating in the entire scenario. Fear of prying Soviet satellites photographing the western desert of the United States obviously persuaded Vaught not to gather his forces in one spot. There is also the strong possibility that the tight training schedule did not allow enough time for all units to converge at one site for a run-through.[17]

Yet General Jones, in his report, stated that "four full-scale scenario rehearsals with all elements of the force . . . were conducted." In fact, as the Holloway panel confirmed, only two C-130s and four H-53s (basically the same model as the RH-53D) had been used to "validate" the Desert One concept. But, said the panel, the plan for the desert rendezvous was "soft" because it never had been properly tested (with *all* elements of the force). When Admiral Holloway's interrogators sought a reason for the omission, they were told that, for reasons of operational security, it was decided not to schedule a full-dress tryout of the Desert One rendezvous. Additionally, the White House propensity for calling alerts, plus the need for compressed training, probably inclined Vaught to decide against the exercise.[18]

This failure to conduct a comprehensive, full-scale training exercise meant that the task force was not completely battle-ready in communications and command and control. Communication is almost always the critical factor in combat operations. If anything goes wrong, chances are that the cause will be traced to faulty communications: messages are sent but not received; or messages are received by a radio operator who fails to pass them on to the commander; or self-imposed communications security can be so limiting that no one, not even the commander, knows how the operation is progressing.

In the case of Vaught's task force, more joint training in communication procedures would have better integrated the force. Apparently, the Holloway investigators had in mind the notable lack of operational control that became obvious during the flight of the helicopters to Desert One. Isolated from the action and troubled by ineffective communications, General Vaught and his subcommanders received scant information and so were unable to make decisions to meet unexpected events.

By ruling out a complete rehearsal at a U.S. training site, Vaught denied himself the opportunity to uncover some of those problems that plagued his force later. According to the panel, a run-through would have surely eliminated such mishaps (traceable to a lack of communications) as the helicopter flight commander's arriving last at Desert One and the deputy commander's aborting the mission. The panel was careful to state, however, that none of its recommendations could have had an effect on the key tragedy of the collision. The point was, rather, that their recommendations might be of significant benefit in future operations.[19]

Missing "Destruct" Devices

One of the major questions swirling around the aborted operation was why the marines failed to destroy the helicopters left behind on the desert. The Holloway investigators asked this same question and added another: Why had not self-destruct grenades been installed on board and the air crews trained in their use? While General Vaught's staff had a plan for destroying the aircraft if need arose, the scheme was limited and proved unusable at Desert One. If destruction became necessary, the commandos were to plant thermite grenades on board and explode them. But as the conflagration raged on, Colonel Kyle evidently decided that using grenades was too risky. Beckwith later explained that the incendiary charges were carried by one of his men, a sergeant. After the explosion, the Deltas, including the sergeant, scattered to board the C-130s. He could not readily be found because, as Beckwith put it, "time ran out." As Kyle saw it, explosions from the helicopters and burning ammunition might well have injured the grenade handlers, the men in the C-130s, and the panicky Iranians in the bus.

Noting the absence of detailed plans for "contingency destruction of equipment" when such equipment might be abandoned in hostile territory, the panel observed that explosives, properly installed, were no more dangerous to the crew than on-board fuel. In postmission interviews, helicopter crewmen were queried as to their reactions if self-destruct grenades had been installed on board. They testified that such a system would have been acceptable to them, but their views had not been sought. In fact, several, if not all, helicopters carried explosives to breach the embassy walls *and* to destroy helicopters, if necessary. Therefore, declared the Holloway panel, it was "a moot point as to what explosives were carried on board or where they were placed."

To reinforce their finding, the investigators stated that

before the SonTay assault in Indochina, the crew had rigged explosives and detonators for helicopter self-destruction, leaving electrical leads disconnected. If the moment came to destroy the helo, the crew could quickly connect the timing device to the explosives and evacuate.

It seems clear that Vaught had not gone far enough in his plan to destroy the helicopters, particularly when they might possibly be abandoned in a hostile country. If self-destruct systems had been installed, flight safety would not have been compromised. There was ample time for crew training. And any helicopter could have been destroyed at any stage in the operation. At Desert One the aircrews could have quickly activated the explosive systems and destroyed all remaining helos. The panel concluded that Colonel Kyle's ability to destroy the aircraft and classified material was "severely limited" by a deficiency that could have been avoided by better planning and a more imaginative approach. The failure of the task force to install destruct devices called forth some of the sharpest criticism in the report.[20]

Fear of Electronic Detection

Concern that the Iranians were capable of monitoring the task force's radio circuits undoubtedly caused the planners in Washington to impose strict radio silence during the helicopter flight to Desert One. To provide some sort of silent communication between helos, the crews were authorized to use hand-held signal lamps that could flash Morse Code or other visual signals. Of course, once the helos entered the dust clouds, these signal lamps became useless. This tight communications procedure prompted the panel to comment that "selected use of radio communications could well have resulted in a more favorable execution of the movement to Desert One." We have already seen how General Vaught's inability to keep abreast of the tactical situation stemmed from this self-imposed radio silence.

It is probable that Vaught's staff had received intelligence reports to the effect that the Iranians possessed equipment capable of picking up electronic signal intelligence (SIGINT). On the other hand, perhaps certain U.S. officers had learned that the Iranians lacked the equipment to pick up signals from sophisticated U.S. transmitters. Members of the Holloway group implied as much in their oblique comment that they would have ensured a "comprehensive and detailed understanding of threat capabilities [posed by Iran's detection equipment] by every member of the [task] force, to include impact and consequences."

In questioning key people, the panel found that the men had varied understandings of the SIGINT threat. Their different understandings affected their decisions, particularly during the harrowing helo flight. In other words, it is likely that the staff did not brief the helicopter aircrews on Iran's SIGINT equipment and the degree of its effectiveness. It is possible that staff officers were so traumatized by the security hobgoblin that they, unwittingly, were less disposed to give the combat team the complete tactical picture, including information on Iran's electronic capabilities. It also may be true that those who made the decisions for the rescue may have been ignorant of current communications technology. To make certain that the U.S. military got the point, the Holloway group urged that future operations take into account "a comprehensive analysis, assessment, and training in matters of SIGSEC [signal security] operations and planning."[21]

The Holloway Group's Recommendations

The deliberations of the panel produced two major recommendations that pointed to significant gaps in the armed forces' ability to mount special operations. First, the Defense Department should establish a counterterrorist task force, with a permanently assigned staff and certain assigned forces, as a field agency of the Joint Chiefs of Staff. Such a task force would provide the president with many options, ranging from a small group of highly trained specialists to a larger joint force.

In its second recommendation, the panel, with memories

of the lack of a "murder board," proposed that the JCS consider the formation of a special operations advisory panel. Its membership would consist of selected senior officers (active or retired) who had served in special operations or as commanders in chief of fleets or forces, or as members of the JCS. The five to seven members would be appointed to serve for no more than three years. The term would be kept relatively short to ensure fresh viewpoints. If a crisis arose that seemed to call for a special operation, several members would review the plans. Their function, the Holloway group emphasized, would be to give the JCS the most objective, independent review possible. Clearly, in future covert operations, any proposal should be scrutinized by outside experts who had not participated in the planning.[22]

An old adage, cited by naval weaponry officers, states that all safety precautions are written in blood. So it was with the findings of Admiral Holloway and his group of generals, who had targeted two basic reasons for the disaster: a trained task force had not been instantly ready, and the JCS had lacked an advisory panel. In identifying the latter shortcoming, the review group strongly implied that any future presidents should listen to a "murder board" before authorizing a covert operation clouded with uncertainties. In 1982, the author was reliably informed that such a board had been appointed and was prepared to act when needed.

8

The Aftermath of the Raid

The Public's Verdict

According to Admiral Holloway, the Joint Chiefs believed that the operation had a 60 to 70 percent chance of success, which meant also that it had a 30 to 40 percent chance of failure. These were not good odds when the lives of fifty-three American hostages were hanging in the balance. We know that, if necessary, Beckwith's Deltas were prepared to see many Iranians die. Once his men were inside the embassy compound, it was certain that the Iranian guards would have been met by a stream of bullets. Hundreds of other Iranians would have been felled if Beckwith had called in the C-130 gunships circling overhead.[1]

We may picture the outburst of international condemnation that would have erupted in protest against such American "brutality." The world would have perceived the rescue operation as a bloodbath, which no amount of diplomatic explanations could have washed away. And what of the two hundred Americans still working freely in Iran? Would infuriated Iranians have set upon these innocent souls, some of whom might have met the fate of U.S. Vice-Consul Robert

} July 1924, this hapless diplomat was stoned
ersian mob in Tehran after being accused by a
…. poisoning a sacred well. He died soon after of his
injuries.[2]

For all Carter's unceasing concern for the hostages, he
appeared not to understand that some problems cannot immediately be solved by the use of force, especially if the chance
of failure was one in three. In spite of the fact that the American public had been dissatisfied with the hostage stalemate, a
majority subsequently disapproved of the rescue attempt.
Public opinion can be a two-edged sword; after the failed
mission, Carter stood censured by an opinion poll which, in
June 1980, found that only 29 percent of the respondents
supported the raid.[3]

The Hostages' Mixed Reactions

On their return from captivity, the hostages expressed different opinions on Carter's decision. Quizzed by the press after
almost fifteen months as a prisoner, Commander Donald
Sharer, a naval aviator, said that he was prepared to endure
imprisonment. He stoutly asserted that the hostages understood why the U.S. government could not allow the lives of
the hostages to be used in a ploy to "jeopardize the lives of 200
million" other Americans. Sharer and some of his colleagues
appreciated that their safety and well-being were secondary to
the national interest.

L. Bruce Laingen, the U.S. chargé d'affaires, who had
been sequestered at the Foreign Affairs Ministry, commented
that it was very difficult to see how the mission could have
resulted in a safe evacuation, given the location of the embassy
within the city, the Iranian guards, the gunmen in the streets,
and the confusing layout of the compound. All of these factors
militated against a casualty-free rescue.

Victor Tomseth, the embassy's political counselor,
agreed with Laingen, adding that the timing of the rescue was
politically inopportune. The operation, as planned, would
have taken place just as Washington was gaining support from

European and Asian nations to impose sanctions on Iran. Tomseth acknowledged that he agreed with unnamed State Department officials in their prediction that if the raid had succeeded, all Americans in Iran would have been thrown in prison.

One hostage, happy that the raid had failed, was quoted as "thanking God for the sandstorm" that had ultimately served to prevent the Deltas from reaching the embassy, with possibly fatal results.

But others approved the raid. Two military officers, Colonel Thomas E. Schaefer, the air force attaché, and Colonel Charles W. Scott, the army attaché, both veterans of Vietnam, supported the idea of the raid. Schaefer recalled that his morale was bolstered because Washington had taken some sort of action. Colonel Scott, for his part, interpreted the aborted mission in terms of a thought attributed to Theodore Roosevelt: "Far better it is to dare mighty things to win glorious triumphs, even though checkered by failure, than to take rank with those poor spirits who neither enjoy much nor suffer much, because they live in the grey twilight that knows not victory nor defeat."[4]

Several other hostages also expressed approval for the try, reflecting a poetic idealism more expressive of individual emotions than of the realistic requirements of U.S. foreign policy or a realistic assessment of the raid. Reportedly, Pentagon sources estimated that as many as thirty of Beckwith's men and fifteen hostages might have been killed in the attempt. Although the task force was forced to return home empty-handed, the nation was spared the pain and travail that inevitably would have resulted if Beckwith's troops had met any resistance.

The Holloway-Beckwith Clash

Rumors that the marine pilots were not fully qualified for the mission came to a head in 1982. In the summer of that year, the British Broadcasting Corporation produced a lengthy analysis of the aborted raid, which was aired on its weekly television

show "Panorama." Separate interviews with Admiral Holloway and Colonel Beckwith unexpectedly engendered much
heat over the performance of the helicopter pilots.[5]

Admiral Holloway, who was interviewed at his
Washington office on 30 July 1982, described the assault as
"brilliantly conceived and well executed" up to the Desert
One stage. "We couldn't have gotten a more competent group
of people together for this operation," he said. He showered
praise on the combat force which performed "absolutely mag-
nificently." The admiral also made clear that if only the services had been immediately prepared to take on this commando mission, they would have been spared the onerous
tasks of screening and training personnel as well as searching
out special equipment from widespread sources.

As a naval aviator who had examined the helicopter
maintenance records, Holloway declared that these eight aircraft were in "Rolls Royce" condition when they took off
from the Nimitz. In his view, only "incredibly bad luck" had
made them the Achilles' heel of the mission. The program
then cut to Colonel Beckwith and his BBC interviewer.
Speaking in a gravelly drawl, the former Green Beret asserted
that the helicopters were not "exercised enough" (that is,
flown under combat conditions). In other words, Beckwith
implied, if the pilots had operated the aircraft sufficiently, they
would have ironed out the defects that eventually grounded
three of the helicopters.

Always one to speak bluntly, Beckwith told his television audience that if he were to repeat the operation, he would
look for the "very best pilots that it took to do the job," a
direct jab at the thirteen marines who made up most of the
sixteen pilots. Beckwith added that, while he was not "putting
anyone down," the helicopter pilots were not up to the state-
of-the-art flying that was expected of them. "There were
people around who were further advanced than these individuals were." Beckwith undoubtedly had in mind special
operations pilots of the air force who were, Beckwith be-

lieved, "more advanced" than the marines in executing covert missions.

When the camera cut to Holloway to whom Beckwith's statement had just been read, the obviously aroused admiral retorted that during the official investigation no one had criticized the helicopter pilots. Admittedly, many of the task force members set forth their "beefs," but not one of them had complained of the helo pilots. "The best pilots in uniform were selected for the job," he said.

Beckwith next was asked if in the heat of action he had called certain individuals "cowards." He answered that if he did use the word, it was meant to stimulate someone to get on with the job. Admiral Holloway, on hearing this passage, shot back that if anyone was now accusing someone of "lack of guts" and had failed to advise the review group, then he, Holloway, "would question his motivation and honesty if he didn't tell us!"

We will recall that the review group had found that, given the urgency in mounting the rescue operation, there was nothing to suggest that any other group of aircrews could have performed the mission better. But the group had noted that those selecting the pilots would have most likely produced the most competent crews more quickly if they had given heavy weight to pilots with air force special operations/rescue or Marine Corps assault experience.[6]

Evidence does not support Beckwith's alleged maligning of brave men. *Newsweek* quoted him as acknowledging that he had used the word to vent his "emotional frustration" and "to stimulate certain personnel to carry out their task." In his book, published two years later, Beckwith again tried to explain his attitude toward the marine pilots. True, he states that on learning that only five helicopters were flyable, he cursed and asked, "Did these pilots want to go, really want to go?" Later, when the group had returned to Masirah, he cautioned his men, "Don't say anything [derogatory] to those pilots. Leave them alone. Don't do or say anything." He goes on to write that at Desert One he never called anyone a coward, but "in Egypt it was a different matter," where he evidently used the epithet in referring to some of the drivers in the group who had left their weapons at Desert One. "At this time," he states, "I may have also called the helo pilots cowards . . . I carried a great deal of stress . . . I am not a perfect person." And he acknowledged that he was wrong.[7]

During the BBC program, the interviewer remarked to Beckwith that in the course of the actual rescue of the embassy personnel, "up to one hundred planes of different kinds could have been available. Sixty aircraft would have been in the air at one time." Beckwith replied,

> If I had got into a situation, based on what I was told by my Commander-in-Chief, the President of the United States, where the success of this operation and the loss of life [were involved]—I would certainly have called in these planes to help me and I think they would have. But there was no plan to go in there and maliciously kill people.

This interchange apparently indicates that both the BBC interviewer and Beckwith assumed that naval carrier planes were ready to be called in to knock out any resistance encountered in Tehran. Media accounts had been illustrated with maps showing how aircraft from the *Nimitz* and another carrier would have supported the operation. There is no question that the C-130 gunships were prepared to act. But evidence that carrier strike planes were part of the operation is wanting. However, plans may have called for a few U.S. Air Force fighter planes to be over Manzariyeh, where the hostages and Delta Force were to board transport aircraft.

The range of carrier aircraft was probably insufficient for them to fly to Tehran, spend thirty minutes over the target, and return to the ship. It is true that the planes could have refueled in flight from aircraft tankers. But such an operation was highly improbable because of its complexity and the large number of tankers required. One may well ask why Colonel Beckwith did not contradict the BBC interviewer when he hinted at sixty naval aircraft. The answer, undoubtedly, is that

Provided in-flight fueling was possible, planes from the *Nimitz* and *Coral Sea*, such as these F-14 Tomcat fighters, could have been sent to the aid of Colonel Beckwith's men. This photograph was taken on board the *Nimitz*. (U.S. Navy)

＿＿n was under wraps not to reveal information or to confirm any supposition by television interviewers.

A Failure in Leadership?

Postmortems concerning the leadership of the operational planning intensified in the two years after the disaster. A common theme was that the planners had failed to sense the enormous distances and the desert conditions involved and had required that men and machines operate on the outer limits of performance. The combination of compartmentation, excessive security, insufficient helicopters, inadequate weather information, and nonuse of pathfinder planes had induced, if not actually caused, the need to operate on the outer limits. Future War College students may well study the Iran raid as an example of how decisionmakers must think long and hard enough about worst-case possibilities before approving any battle plan.[8]

Another criticism of the Pentagon's leadership came from retired Major General John Singlaub, known in the army for his exploits in special operations. Reportedly, Singlaub had been called to the Pentagon to explore ways to improve special operations following the misfortune in Iran. In 1982, Singlaub appeared on the same BBC program as Admiral Holloway and Colonel Beckwith. Responding to a question on the role of each service in the assault, Singlaub surprisingly replied: "There were some political considerations. I think that an effort was made to get *all* of the services involved," by which he implied that marine helo pilots were brought into the operation (rather than air force pilots trained in special operations) to permit marine corps participation. He went on to say that an operation in which marine pilots flew navy helicopters and carried army troops supported by the air force "had a nice ring to it, in a public-relations sense." But if this arrangement was a factor, and "there were some who thought it was a major factor," then, he said, "it was wrong."[9]

However, Colonel J. L. McManaway, USMC, states that "a member of the JCS [at the time of the raid, General

Robert H. Barrow, USMC (Ret.)] tells me that all services were given a chance to supply pilots for the rescue attempt. Marines, navy, and air force [helicopter] pilots finally flew on the raid, having been found the best qualified to fly the aircraft during the training period." Colonel McManaway, who talked to members of the task force, states that all of the marine pilots were handpicked and the majority were veterans of at least one tour in Vietnam.

Singlaub believed that the rescue failed because it had been hurriedly organized. The Pentagon, he explained, no longer had available men who had trained, planned, and worked together during past years. The rescue did not succeed because, basically, "we tried to bring disparate units from all over the Armed Forces, from all over the world—and then put them into an ad hoc arrangement to do a very complicated plan."

Dr. Brzezinski, one of the prime movers of the operation, voiced no regrets over the leadership. Instead, he blamed mechanical difficulties for the blunders. "Little did I dream that our failure would involve technology, an area where America normally excels," he recalled.[10]

Admiral Turner's Call for an Inquiry

Two years after the raid Admiral Stansfield Turner, who as head of the CIA, had participated in the planning, proposed that a new investigation be conducted. Now retired from public life, Turner was quoted in an interview by a *Washington Post* journalist as stating that the raid had not been completely reviewed for the lessons it held.[11]

In rebuttal, General Jones replied that an inquiry would serve no useful purpose because there was little about the raid that had not already been explored. Jones, whom the *Post* writer described as the "principal architect of the rescue mission," argued that the Iranian raid situation would never be repeated. "We don't need to go back and look at things that happened two years ago," he said, pointing out that Admiral Holloway's group already had issued a critical report.

Admiral Stansfield Turner before he became director of the CIA and a member of the Special Coordinating Committee involved in the Tehran rescue mission. Two years after the aborted raid, Admiral Turner called for a detailed investigation of the episode, specifically with regard to the nation's command system. (U.S. Navy)

Later, in August 1983, Admiral Turner commented that it would be most unfortunate for the nation "to go through a trauma like this" and not try to determine if the failed mission held important lessons for the future. He went on to say:

> What I have in mind is someone to look at our overall capability for lower threshold operations such as this; how we motivate our military officers and men today in the light of a number of indications of less than full perseverance in this instance; whether the performance of our equipment was satisfactory and whether the military truly understands their limitations or believes the brochures of the manufacturers; how good our military training and planning procedures are in light of the military's inability to come up with a reasonable, operational capability for a number of months after the capture of the hostages; and others.
>
> My hope would be that a President would appoint a very small panel of senior, distinguished citizens—perhaps three or four—who would be given full access to the records of this event. The people would work quietly and out of the spotlight in an attempt to come up with both a classified and an unclassified report as to whether any major adjustments in our military procedures, and in our national security procedures were warranted.[12]

These recommendations made by a senior official, intimately associated with the high-level planning of the operation, did not prevail over General Jones's opinion. The secret Holloway report represents, so far as is publicly known, the only official investigation.

Lessons Learned

The Desert One episode demonstrated to the American public, and the Reagan administration in particular, that the so-called special forces (Navy Seals, Air Force Special Operations units, and the Army Green Berets), *if properly used*, possess unique abilities to rescue and protect U.S. citizens and property overseas when foreign governments, terrorists, or insurgents posed a threat. Because the special forces have mobility, flexibility, and speed, the president could respond fast whenever the need arose.

According to Pentagon observers, an additional benefit, stemming from the raid, was the restored status of the Chiefs

One month after the tragedy of Desert One, President Carter welcomed the crew of the carrier *Nimitz* upon her return from the Indian Ocean. Eight helicopters had lifted off from the carrier for the flight to Desert One. (U.S. Navy)

as direct military advisors to the president. From the Kennedy administration in 1960 through the Carter years, the Chiefs's legal role as military advisors to the commander in chief became one in name only because the respective presidents, by choice, saw the Chiefs only at infrequent, general meetings and not in private consultation. Advice from the Chiefs was funneled through the defense secretary, who may or may not have transmitted the exact sense to the chief executive.

This tenuous tie with the White House changed in the fall of 1982, when the Chiefs sought and were encouraged to meet with the president regularly. Once again, after a twenty-year hiatus, the president consulted face to face with the nation's most competent military minds.

9

Desert One and
Other Special Operations

The United States, the most powerful nation on earth, has on occasion found it difficult to protect its people abroad or on the high seas. One reason for this paradox was that many in government and many Americans generally were slow to comprehend that massive nuclear forces, fleets, and armies, while suitable in preventing all-out war, were not appropriate in dealing with the sort of conflicts that characterized the 1960s and 1970s—incidents of hijacking, kidnapping, assassination, and bombing. There is a need to design our military so that it will be best able to respond to the most likely challenges of the future.

There is also a need to fit the Iranian hostage rescue attempt into historical perspective. Similar episodes of the recent past illustrate both the strengths and weaknesses of the U.S. armed forces, and an understanding of those elements allows us to capitalize on our strengths and tells us what we need to improve.

On the positive side is the courage, resolution, and individual competence of U.S. combat men. Even these military virtues, however, cannot carry the day if the command system is flawed, as it was during the Bay of Pigs episode.

The Bay of Pigs Landing

The inglorious Cuban invasion is a classic example of how a great nation can fail spectacularly in carrying out a relatively small-scale mission. In April 1961, in a move to upset Fidel Castro's regime in Cuba, President John F. Kennedy decided to support an invasion by fifteen hundred anti-Castro commandos. Unwisely, he assigned control of this combat mission to civilian officials at the Central Intelligence Agency.

The plan called for the Free Cubans to make an amphibious landing on the south coast at the Bay of Pigs (Bahia Cochinos). In a misguided move to conceal Washington's role in the operation, Kennedy directed that the Joint Chiefs of Staff be kept isolated from the plan.

On 17 April 1961, as the Free Cubans waded ashore, they came under strafing attack from Castro's aircraft. Since Kennedy had forbidden any combat flights by the invaders' air squadron, their ships were soon sunk or damaged and all fifteen hundred men either killed or captured. Castro's victory was an arresting example of why an amphibious force must, first, establish control of the air before attempting a landing.

Ironically, the U.S. carrier *Essex* was on station off the Bay of Pigs with its attack planes ready for takeoff to support the landing. But the order to launch aircraft never came because Kennedy had rejected all urgings by the Joint Chiefs to release the navy jets to save the Free Cubans. Despite all the signs to the contrary, he adamantly maintained that the United States should appear not to be involved.[1]

Kennedy's failure in this case is a grim reminder that a commander-in-chief, once he decides on a course of action, must have the will to use sufficient military force to attain his objective. Furthermore, when a commander selects an objective, it must be clearly defined and militarily achievable. And when a plan is devised, it must be relatively simple and concise to avoid confusion and misinterpretation. Measured against these imperatives, the Bay of Pigs operation reveals its inherent defects.[2]

The Capture of the USS *Pueblo*

Six years after the Bay of Pigs fiasco, the seizure of the USS *Pueblo* persuaded foreign observers that, once again, the United States had acted like a paper tiger. On 23 January 1968, several North Korean ships surrounded and seized the U.S. vessel on the high seas. The small *Pueblo* was loaded with secret electronic intelligence-collection equipment that recorded foreign radio and radar transmissions. The eighty-three crew members were thrown into prison on charges of spying in North Korean waters.

Pressed by the Congress to explain why the *Pueblo* had been positioned so close to North Korean, the Defense Department disclosed that several federal organizations, including the supersecret National Security Agency, the Pentagon, and elements of the Pacific Fleet, were all involved in directing the ship's movements. The chain of responsibility had become fragmented, so much so, in fact, that the Pacific Fleet commander and his subordinates lacked authority to change the *Pueblo*'s route without first checking with Washington. It was also true that the ship's captain was at fault by failing to react to obvious signs of danger and to clear the area in time. Why had not U.S. forces responded to the *Pueblo*'s call for help? The answer was that all U.S. ships and planes were too distant to render timely aid.

With the *Pueblo* in North Korean hands, President Lyndon Johnson, already deep in a conflict in Indochina, decided that he could not risk a second war, and he negotiated a humane but humiliating settlement. At home, many Americans expressed outrage that their powerful country seemed helpless to protect the freedom of the seas, a fundamental principle of U.S. foreign policy ever since Lieutenant Stephen Decatur first fought the Barbary pirates in 1804.

In hindsight, we can see that the overly complex line of command and the lack of coordination between Washington and the Pacific Command pointed to a ponderous bureaucracy that diluted command responsibility. It is not a new problem in U.S. history. A similar situation occurred in the months before Pearl harbor, when Washington bureaucrats withheld valuable intelligence on Japanese intentions from the U.S. Hawaiian commanders for reasons of security.[3]

The *Mayaguez* Incident

The *Mayaguez* incident, in contrast to other recent crises involving capture of U.S. citizens and property, stands out as an example of swift presidential action and resolution. On 12 May 1975, the *Mayaguez*, a 10,000-ton cargo ship of U.S. registry, was fired on and captured by Cambodian communists while steaming off the Cambodian coast. The seizure came shortly after the hasty departure of American diplomats from Saigon and the pell-mell evacuation by thousands of Indochinese refugees fleeing a conquering North Vietnamese army.

Faced with his first major crisis, President Ford immediately directed the JCS to devise a rescue plan. He was told to expect between twenty and forty casualties. (As matters turned out, forty-one American combat men lost their lives.) Fortunately, the *Mayaguez* had radioed an SOS, together with its position, before being captured. Within hours a U.S. Navy Orion patrol plane had located the ship. In the meantime, the carrier *Coral Sea*, en route to Australia, and two destroyers in the Philippines area, were ordered to intercept the captured ship. At the U.S. base on Okinawa, a marine battalion landing team boarded air force transports and flew to an airfield in Thailand that would serve as a staging point.[4]

On 13 May, a patrol plane pilot flying off the Cambodian coast reported the *Mayaguez* to be anchored off Tang Island, presumably with its crew aboard. Actually, the Cambodians had transferred the crew of forty to a fishing boat and sailed for the mainland thirty-four miles distant. The tempo of events quickened.

In the next twenty-four hours planes from the *Coral Sea* attacked Cambodian ships and targets ashore, destroying seventeen aircraft, buildings, a runway, and three gunboats.

Marines from a destroyer, the *Harold E. Holt*, recaptured the *Mayaguez*, finding the ship deserted. Simultaneously, another group of marines landed at nearby Tang Island where some 150 communists were entrenched. Naval aircraft struck the enemy positions but could not prevent a bloody firefight from breaking out, in which both sides suffered casualties. By day's end the marines were evacuated by helicopter to the waiting U.S. naval ships.

On the morning of 15 May, a patrol plane reported that a small fishing boat, with mostly Caucasians on board, was headed for Tang Island. A destroyer, the *Henry B. Wilson*, came alongside, removed all forty crewmen, and transported them to the undamaged *Mayaguez*, which was soon underway. As the *Mayaguez* captain explained, after the carrier strike, the Cambodians had prudently decided to set them free.

Some might argue that if Ford had negotiated with the Cambodians, he might well have won the release of the crew. Others, more skeptical, were aware that the Pol Pot regime, which ruled Cambodia, had tortured and murdered thousands. Consequently, there was every chance that negotiations would have led to a repetition of the degrading *Pueblo* agreement, by which the U.S. government had signed an apology for the alleged intrusion in North Korean waters. As soon as the men were set free, Washington repudiated the document.

With the *Pueblo* lesson in mind, President Ford did not hesitate when circumstances called for military force. His action was a vivid demonstration of what might happen to other nations which did not respect U.S. lives and property in international waters.

For all its quick success, the *Mayaguez* affair exposed the need for a fast-reaction, multiservice counterterrorist force. Such a force would have eliminated much of the extemporaneous, ad hoc element in the rescue. A special command, with its own air transport, helicopters, and assault teams, could have been on the scene within twenty-four hours. In

1975, however, few officials in Washington were paying attention to the growth of international terrorism—on the sea or on land—and to the need of such a special force.

The valiant performance of the marines, the aviators (both navy and air force), and the destroyer crews, who rendered fire-support at Tang Island, testified to the professional competence of the individual services. Unhappily, Washington leaders could not resist the temptation to control operations via telephone communication. One patrol squadron commander later recalled that he and other officers were disrupted in their work by constant calls from seniors asking for status reports, presumably in response to White House demands.

In 1980, Ford contrasted the *Mayaguez* rescue with the Iran hostage crisis. Central to each incident was the need to convey to the world a sense of U.S. armed might and the determination to use it. According to Ford, a key element in any crisis is time. "Time is not on your side . . . time dictates the decision to move . . . time does not give you more opportunities, but less."[5]

A New Look at Special Operations Forces

Events at Desert One undoubtedly caused the JCS to give higher priority to the study of unconventional warfare and the strengthening of a joint, unconventional, special-warfare force drawn from all three services. In 1982, the Joint Chiefs, some of whom were newly appointed, disclosed that they fully intended to press for improvement of the special forces. In a study for the Congress on military posture for fiscal year 1983, the JCS stated:

> The current special operations forces levels reflect a serious shortfall in the number and types of units to meet requirements now and in the remainder of the decade. To offset this critical shortfall, a measured expansion of special operations forces is required.[6]

A year later, the Chiefs informed the Congress that they had established a joint command to improve the effectiveness of special operations forces. Areas receiving attention were the following: development of joint operational doctrine; coordination of training; development of specialized equipment that could be operated by qualified personnel regardless of service branch; and improvement in structure of the special forces. Evidence of the strengthening of the counterterrorist forces surfaced again in early 1983 with the announcement that the Army Special Forces would be expanded by one third.[7]

But one former member of the Joint Staff was less than optimistic. Some four years after the rescue attempt, Lieutenant General John S. Pustay, who had helped to plan the Desert One mission, charged that the resources assigned to the development and coordination of unconventional warfare elements were "modest," an indication that JCS and congressional support fell short of solving the problem.

General Pustay, now retired, was an assistant to the JCS chairman in 1980 and had participated in the secret meetings of Dr. Brzezinski's committee. Writing in the *Armed Forces Journal*, Pustay listed various deficiencies in the rescue attempt. Basically, the armed forces lacked a joint force trained to meet situations caused by state-supported terrorism and guerrilla warfare. This weakness forced the Joint Chiefs "to artificially join together disparate elements from the Services to carry out a complex anti-terrorist mission." While such Yankee ingenuity may have been admirable, Pustay pointed out that it also highlights the high command's lack of attention to so-called lower-level conflicts.

Pustay revealed two reasons why the Iranian rescue mission was supervised by "the highest authorities in Washington. First, the U.S. commanders in chief in Europe and in the Pacific, because their staffs did not include officers skilled in antiterrorism and because their subordinate commands lacked units qualified in combined special-warfare missions, were not prepared to mount an unconventional operation on the scale of Desert One. Second, the "sensitive nature" of the Iranian raid persuaded "the highest authorities" to assume the role of supervisors.

The lesson of Desert One, Pustay made clear, was that

until the military high command (and the Congress) developed a "joint perspective" in dealing with combat situations, including unconventional warfare, the armed forces would be plagued by foul-ups such as those that marked Desert One. He predicted that the armed forces would lack a joint perspective until the JCS organization was strengthened to eliminate single-service thinking and until "many entrenched forces" accepted the idea of joint structuring of the armed forces.[8]

There is a veiled suggestion in General Pustay's words that, during the planning of the Iran mission, General Jones and Pustay may have encountered "single service" thinking and even resistance from certain quarters. Even though Jones was the JCS chairman, under existing law, he could exercise no military command over the Chiefs or the unified commanders. Historians must wait for more evidence before concluding that the plan may have been weakened, first, by the chairman's inability to exercise direct control over the services and, second, by well-meant but unsuitable instructions by Washington's "highest authorities."

Epilogue

Proposals for Change

The Grenada Landing—Leaving the Military Alone

Some two years after the Desert One disaster, the armed forces were again called on to enforce U.S. foreign policy. Two interventions, one in Grenada and the other in Beirut, produced conflicting opinions as to whether Washington leaders had taken to heart all the lessons learned from the failed rescue mission in Iran.

The Grenada operation, labeled by Reagan's critics as an "invasion," and by his supporters as a "rescue," was triggered when senior Grenadian officers assassinated Prime Minister Maurice Bishop as well as cabinet members and innocent civilians on 19 October 1983. The killers, Moscow-oriented extremists who wanted closer ties with the Soviet Union, quickly seized power and proclaimed a shoot-on-sight curfew.

The murdered Bishop, a Marxist lawyer, had led his country into a Soviet-Cuban web when he had engineered his own takeover in 1979 with the aid of Cuban commandos. Generous economic and military aid from Moscow, coupled with the establishment of heavily staffed Soviet and Cuban embassies on the island, culminated in a project to build a 10,000-foot airfield. Significantly, Bishop had signed pacts permitting Soviet and Cuban aircraft and ships to use the airfield and Grenadian ports. Unwittingly, he had brought on his assassination when he decided to loosen his ties with Moscow.[1]

The Kremlin's presence in Grenada naturally was a subject of concern to the Reagan administration. A Soviet-dominated Grenada could serve not only as a valuable logistics station for long-range reconnaissance planes and submarines but also as a base to train guerrillas in subversion methods that could be exported to neighboring islands. Moreover, the JCS was particularly conscious of the navy's need to transit the Panama Canal and to control the Caribbean sea lanes through which passed more than fifty percent of the oil consumed by the United States.

The menace of the brutal new regime prompted Grenada's island-neighbors, all of which were former British colonies, to seek military help from President Reagan to preserve the peace and safety of the eastern Caribbean. At the same time, Washington rightly feared for the safety of one thousand Americans, including several hundred medical school students, who were residents on the island and might well be seized—Tehran-style—as hostages. An urgent plea for a U.S. military rescue also came from Grenada's governor general, the British Crown's representative on the island.[2]

Concerned that swift action was called for, Reagan did not commit the error of employing too little force too late. Within three days, the Joint Chiefs had ordered a naval task force, then en route to the Mediterranean, to be diverted to Grenada. The landing took place at dawn on 25 October 1983. To give the force a multinational character, the task force included police units from Jamaica and other Caribbean states.[3]

Some 5,500 U.S. Army personnel and 500 marines were opposed by 2,000 Grenadian and 450 Cuban soldiers, but within a week the U.S. and Caribbean forces had prevailed.

Fatalities comprised 160 Grenadians and 71 Cuban troops, and 18 U.S. combatants. Eighteen civilians also died when carrier aircraft, in an attack on Grenada's Fort Benjamin, unintentionally destroyed a mental hospital adjacent to this command post. Contrary to custom, the hospital was not marked with a distinctive red cross which might have prevented the attack.[4]

The success of the Grenada mission indicated a change in U.S. military operations—from the beginning, there was a conscious decision by the White House that there would be no second-guessing by civilian officials. Admiral Wesley McDonald, the Atlantic commander, was in overall charge. His task force commander, Vice Admiral Joseph Metcalf, was assigned a simple military objective with no crippling conditions attached.[5]

Geographic circumstances favored the landings. Grenada was situated relatively close to bases in Panama, Puerto Rico, Florida, and Guantanamo, Cuba. Airports in Barbados and Jamaica were readily available for the use of U.S. airborne units.

Fortunately, the U.S. landing force encountered no hostility from the Grenadian people, who were openly grateful. Nor were their hopes for American generosity misplaced. One month after the landing, Congress approved $15 million in economic aid for the island as the start of a long-range assistance program.

U.S. public opinion, in general, favored the president's action. Partisan Democrats, on the other hand, criticized the landing for various reasons. Historian Arthur Schlesinger, once a member of the Kennedy White House staff, called it a "sneak attack" that was in violation of the charters of the United Nations and the Organization of American States. And a *New York Times* editorial writer, suspicious of the administration's intentions, demanded evidence of Soviet-Cuban influence in Grenada.[6]

As matters turned out, evidence of the Soviet-Cuban presence was ample, as almost 900 foreign "advisors" were rounded up, among them 638 Cubans, plus Russians, North

Koreans, Libyans, East Germans, and Bulgarians. Some were military men. Captured equipment included heavy construction machinery for work at the airport, Soviet armored vehicles, artillery pieces, rocket launchers, hand weapons, and tons of ammunition.

Equally startling was the discovery of five secret military assistance agreements with Moscow, North Korea, and Cuba. Another document confirmed Soviet intentions to convert Grenada into a logistics base and a training center for guerrillas. Other papers revealed that Castro planned to station a force of 341 officers and 4,000 soldiers on the island.[7]

By moving fast, Reagan had demonstrated to the Soviet Union and Cuba that encroachments in the Caribbean would not be tolerated. No longer could Moscow and Havana assume that the area was ripe for takeover.

The Grenada success was not without operational flaws. The press, for instance, reported that for all the navy's "high-tech" communications equipment, its ships could not receive badly needed maps of the island by facsimile transmission from Washington. Allegedly, to get the crucial maps to the fleet, the Pentagon had to have them flown from Washington to Barbados and, thence, to the flagship. The Navy Department's Office of Information declined to comment on the report when asked for details. It is possible, however, that the task force flagship had not been fitted with facsimile equipment but that it would be during a future refit.[8]

The Beirut Bombing

If the Grenada operation was a triumph, the American venture into the war-torn Middle East underlined two military shortcomings. First, both Washington and senior U.S. commanders in Europe exhibited a lack of understanding of antiterrorist tactics. And, second, the chain of command appeared, once again, to be less than clear.

The U.S. involvement in Lebanon began in September 1982, when President Reagan ordered some nineteen hundred marines to be stationed in Beirut as peacekeepers. U.S. interest in Lebanon and the Middle East stemmed from the administration's determination to prevent any cutoff of Middle East oil for NATO Europe, Japan, and the United States. According to Reagan, if Lebanon fell to forces hostile to the West, then the stability of the entire Middle East would be threatened.[9]

Part of a multinational force which included British, French, and Italian troops, the marines were to provide a "presence" that would allow the shaky Lebanese government time to become stabilized. Acting as buffer against warring factions of Shiite Moslems, Christians, Druze Moslems, and other dissidents, the marines became a ready target for terrorists.

On 23 October 1983, a suicidal driver, said to be a Shiite Moslem, drove a truck loaded with munitions equal to twelve thousand pounds of TNT, past marine sentries guarding the compound, straight into the headquarters building. The tremendous explosion killed 241 men.

In the ensuing uproar, administration critics charged that the marines had been sent on a mission that was impossible to carry out; that they had been "sitting ducks" for a year; and that they should be recalled to ships of the Sixth Fleet to assume their proper role in amphibious warfare. In a gesture reminiscent of President Carter, President Reagan publicly acknowledged that responsibility for the affair rested with him and, presumably, not the military officers involved.[10]

Also, as happened after the Desert One debacle, the administration named an investigative commission, this one headed by retired Admiral Robert L. J. Long, who had recently retired as commander in chief, Pacific.★ Unlike the Holloway review group, which concerned itself only with military factors, the Long Commission probed into military matters and foreign policy negotiating tactics, as well.

★The commission members: Robert J. Murray, a former under secretary of the navy; Lieutenant General L. F. Snowden, USMC (Ret); Lieutenant General E. E. Tighe, USAF (Ret); and Lieutenant General J. T. Palastra, USA.

The commission did not mince words in its finding that the officials, who had placed the marines in a plainly hazardous situation, apparently were ignorant of the history of Middle East terrorism. These unnamed U.S. officials had assumed that no one would make the ultimate sacrifice by killing himself in a kamikaze assault on U.S. troops. Throughout the commission report runs the theme that President Reagan and his advisors had given insufficient thought and attention to the safety of the marines and had wrongly assumed that they could protect themselves against any threat. Similarly, throughout the chain of command, there was no clear definition of the meaning of "presence" for the marines, nor were the responsibilities of the marine commander clearly spelled out regarding the security of the Beirut airport.

Thus, with the best of intentions, the high command had set in motion unlooked-for events likely to bring on a deadly bombing. The investigators pulled no punches, identifying, not by name but their command titles, General Bernard Rogers, commander of U.S. Forces, Europe; Vice Admiral William Small, commander, U.S. Naval Forces, Europe; Vice Admiral Edward Martin, commander, Sixth Fleet; and Captain Morgan France, the commander of the Sixth Fleet's amphibious squadron to which the marines were officially attached.[11]

The commission found that these officers "did not initiate actions to effectively ensure the security of the Marines." As the investigation continued, it became clear that General Rogers's antiterrorist experts had been sent to Lebanon to evaluate the bombing of the U.S. Embassy in April 1983 and to recommend steps to prevent a recurrence. Yet, tragically, no one on Rogers' staff had taken any action to conduct a similar protective evaluation of the marine headquarters building, even though the marines were part of his command. Nor did any other senior commander express any apprehension over the possibility of a devastating attack and take steps to meet the threat.[12]

Surprisingly, General Rogers's specialist for security matters, the same officer who had evaluated the embassy bombing, had predicted that this incident would be the prelude to an even more spectacular attack in Beirut, with the U.S. military (the marines) being the logical target. It should be recognized however, that even if the Marines had received such information, they might not have been able to prevent the attempt, so resourceful were the terrorists in penetrating the defenses. Nevertheless, the marines should have received this vital report on the embassy bombing from General Rogers's staff.

Equally regrettable, the commission found that the marines lacked daily, concrete intelligence on terrorist operations. While Colonel Timothy Geraghty, the marine commander, received a flood of intelligence warnings, he was not sent timely reports. Nor did he have intelligence experts attached to his force who could evaluate for him the many reports pouring in. In brief, senior commanders had expressed little or no concern over Middle East terrorist tactics and, in effect, had assumed, wrongly, that the marines could defend themselves.[13]

Possibly the senior commanders were reluctant to counsel the marine commander on antiterrorist measures. If so, they erred. It is well recognized in the military that a tactical commander in the forward area needs essential support. According to the commission, Colonel Geraghty did not receive such assistance and was, therefore, severely restricted in carrying out his mission. Specifically, there was no aggressive command follow-up nor was there continuing command assessment of the task assigned to him or of the support that he required.

"Military commanders are responsible for the performance of their subordinates." This ancient military precept, as stated in the report, formed the basis of the commission's findings. A commander might delegate *authority* to his marine officer subordinate, but a commander could not delegate his *responsibility* for the performance of any of the forces under his command. This theme of command authority and responsibility guided the commission throughout its investigation.[14]

A Change in the Line of Command

Despite criticism of military shortcomings evident in the Beirut mission, the Long report did not suggest that the U.S. high command structure was defective. Nevertheless, the varying degrees of weaknesses evident in three successive operations in Iran, Grenada, and Beirut raised questions on Capitol Hill concerning command and control of the field forces.*

In 1983, a congressional proposal (the Nichols bill) was introduced to place the chairman of the Joint Chiefs in the chain directly under the secretary of defense but over the field commanders. The Nichols bill would give the chairman the power to supervise these commanders and to act as their spokesman on operational requests. Further, the bill would make the chairman a member of the National Security Council. Consequently, the military, after a long interval, would be accorded a formal voice in those diplomatic–political decisions which the armed services would be required to carry out.

In late 1983, the Joint Chiefs gave their full support to the proposed legislation. Presumably Congress and the Pentagon were aware that our postwar operations in unconventional war had exposed certain organizational frailties which were not consistent with America's immense strength.[15]

The world has changed and state-supported terrorism around the globe is but one of these changes that must shape U.S. military thinking. There will be more Grenadas and Beirut-like crises. To meet them we need a joint force, mobile and skilled in unconventional warfare, directed by a national command system that has the will, the authority, and the flexibility to effectively direct its field commanders when hard decisions must be made.

---

*Unified commands comprise: Europe, Atlantic, Pacific, Southern (Latin America), Readiness Command, and Central Command. Specified commands comprise: Aerospace Defense, Strategic Air Command, and Military Airlift Command.

Notes

Chapter 1

1. The number was reduced to fifty-two when Richard Queen, a consular officer, was released because of illness. The Iranians wanted no American to die in captivity.

2. General David C. Jones, "Report on Rescue Mission" (hereafter Jones Report), photocopy, dated 6 May 1980, contains a summary. See also *Time*, 5 May 1982, pp. 12–25; *Newsweek*, 5 May 1980, pp. 27–36; Jimmy Carter, *Keeping Faith: Memoirs of a President* (New York: Bantam Books, 1982), pp. 509–10; and Colonel Charlie A. Beckwith and Donald Knox, *Delta Force* (New York: Harcourt Brace Jovanovich, 1983), pp. 5–10, 220, 253–56.

3. *Newsweek*, 12 July 1982, p. 18; *Aerospace Daily*, 29 April 1980, pp. 328–29; *Aviation Week and Space Technology* (hereafter *Aviation Week*), 5 May 1980, pp. 22–23; Scott Armstrong, George C. Wilson, and Bob Woodward, "Debate Rekindles on Failed Iran Raid," *Washington Post*, 25 April 1982, p. A1.

4. The Entebbe rescue took place on 3 July 1976 and Mogadishu on 13 October 1977. The *Mayaguez* rescue began on 12 May 1975, when President Ford demonstrated to the world that he was not reluctant to use force promptly to rescue U.S. seamen from Cambodian communists.

5. Carter, *Keeping Faith*, p. 518; Carter's statement (photocopy) released by White House, 25 April 1980.

6. *U.S. News & World Report*, 14 April 1980, p. 19. *New York Times*,

25 June 1979, p. 1, reports results of *Times*/CBS poll showing only 20 percent favored Carter's conduct of foreign policy.

7. "Report on Rescue Mission," photocopy, obtained from Defense Department, pp. 63–64; hereafter Holloway Report.

8. Zbigniew Brzezinski, "The Failed Mission," *New York Times Magazine*, 18 April 1982, section 6, pp. 28–79. See also his memoirs, *Power and Principle: Memoirs of the National Security Adviser* (New York: Farrar, Straus, Giroux, 1983), pp. 477–500.

9. Hamilton Jordan, *Crisis: The Last Year of the Carter Presidency* (New York: G. P. Putnam's Sons, 1982); Carter, *Keeping Faith*; Cyrus Vance, *Hard Choices: Critical Years in America's Foreign Policy* (New York: Simon & Schuster, 1983).

10. For an evaluation of Carter's Iran policy by veteran diplomat George Ball, see *Time*, 15 January 1979, p. 25.

11. For Washington's misperception of fervent Islamic nationalism, see John D. Stempel, *Inside the Iranian Revolution* (Bloomington: Indiana University Press, 1981); Michael Ledeen and William Lewis, *Debacle: The American Failure in Iran* (New York: Alfred A. Knopf, 1981); and Barry Rubin, *Paved with Good Intentions: The American Experience and Iran* (New York: Oxford University Press, 1980).

12. *Time*, 12 February 1979, pp. 33–38, describes the turbulence in Tehran. For Washington's misreading of the signs of danger, see Ledeen and Lewis, *Debacle*, pp. 215–17.

13. Ledeen and Lewis, *Debacle*, pp. 175–93; Stempel, *Inside the Iranian Revolution*, pp. 183–88; and Carter, *Keeping Faith*, p. 452.

14. Carter, *Keeping Faith*, p. 451; *Time*, 18 October 1982, p. 57; President's News Conference, 28 November 1979, printed in Department of State *Bulletin*, January 1980, pp. 1–4.

15. Carter, *Keeping Faith*, pp. 455–57. According to Hamilton Jordan, "We felt it was important to have a representation on the ground in Iran. We knew it was a risk but we thought it was a reasonable risk." (Quoted in Robert D. McFadden et al., *No Hiding Place* [New York: Times Books, 1981], pp. 160–63.

16. *U.S. News & World Report*, 19 November 1975, p. 20; Ledeen and Lewis, *Debacle*, pp. 220–24; Carter, *Keeping Faith*, p. 453, explains that he reduced the embassy staff from eleven hundred to some seventy-five and counted on Iranian government to protect the latter.

17. *U.S. News & World Report*, 19 November 1975, p. 25; and Paul B. Ryan, *First Line of Defense: The U.S. Navy since 1945* (Stanford: Hoover Institution Press, 1981), pp. 44–45, p. 164.

18. Department of State *Bulletin*, January 1980, p. 4.

19. Ibid., p. 51, reports that the U.N. Security Council passed a resolution on 25 November 1979 deploring the use of force and calling on Tehran and Washington to find a peaceful solution.

20. Carter, *Keeping Faith*, pp. 459, 496, 506; and *Time*, 18 October 1982, p. 64. Hamilton Jordan, appearing on Phil Donahue's television show, recounted White House fear that Iran might execute one hostage per day and the president's "emotional obsession" to get the hostages out (see "Donahue Transcript" #09282, 1982, pp. 3, 19).

21. Terence Smith, "Putting the Hostages' Lives First," in McFadden, *No Hiding Place*, p. 214.

22. Vance, *Hard Choices*, pp. 408–9. *New York Times*, 16 April 1980, pp. 1, 10, 12; *U.S. News & World Report*, 2 February 1981, pp. 32–33, describes conditions at the U.S. Embassy in Tehran; Scott Blakey, *Prisoner at War: The Survival of Commander Richard A. Stratton* (New York: Doubleday, Anchor Press, 1978) and Jim & Sybil Stockdale, *In Love and War* (New York: Harper and Row, 1984) are vivid accounts of life in a North Vietnamese prison. See also McFadden, *No Hiding Place*, pp. 90–96, 119–25; Carter, *Keeping Faith*, pp. 480–81; Richard Queen with Patricia Hass, *Inside and Out* (New York: G. P. Putnam's Sons, 1981); and James Bond Stockdale, "The Hostages as 'Extortionist-Theater,'" *Washington Post*, 25 January 1981, pp. 6–7.

23. For a chronological account, see *Newsweek*, 9 February 1981, pp. 28–40; *Time*, 18 October 1982; Brzezinski, "The Failed Mission," pp. 28, 29.

24. Brzezinski, "The Failed Mission," p. 29.

25. *Who's Who in America, 1982–83* (Chicago: Marquis Who's Who, 1982), 1:436.

26. Ledeen and Lewis, *Debacle*, p. 236; James Fallows, "Zbig without Cy," *New Republic*, 10 May 1980, p. 18 (Fallows was Carter's chief speech writer in 1977 and 1978); Defense Secretary Harold Brown, news conference, 29 April 1980, p. 1, transcript available from Defense Department; Hamilton Jordan, *Crisis*, p. 49.

27. Brzezinski, "The Failed Mission," pp. 30–31.

28. Ibid., pp. 28–29.

Chapter 2

1. *Who's Who in America, 1980–81* (Chicago: Marquis Who's Who, 1981), 1: 3376; *The Citadel Alumni News*, Fall 1977, p. 1.

2. Beckwith and Knox, *Delta Force*, pp. 181, 194.

3. News conference, Defense Secretary Brown and General Jones, Pentagon, 29 April 1980, pp. 1–2; Report by Congressional Research Service, Library of Congress: "Iran: Consequences of the Abortive Attempt to Rescue the American Hostages," 2 May 1980, pp. 4–5 (photocopy available at Library of Congress); Beckwith and Knox, *Delta Force*, p. 236.

4. "The Iran Raid: Operation Blue Light, an Air Crew Member's Story," *Gung-Ho*, January 1983, pp. 27–30. (This first-person article was

purportedly the first of its kind to appear in print.) See also *Washington Post*, 25 April 1982, p. A14.

5. Holloway Report, pp. vi, 15, 18–20, 60.

6. Brzezinski, "The Failed Mission," p. 29.

7. Ibid., pp. 11, 12, 23.

8. For an account of General Gast's controversial role in Tehran during 1979 as chief, Military Advisory and Assistance Group (MAAG), see Ledeen and Lewis, *Debacle*, pp. 188–89, 192–93, 215, 222–28; *Time*, 18 October 1982, p. 50; and Holloway Report, pp. 15–17, 58. See also Beckwith and Knox, *Delta Force*, p. 204.

9. Holloway Report, pp. 21–22. Surprisingly, the report states, "To the best of the review group's knowledge, no final plan for the rescue operation was ever published prior to mission execution." See also Beckwith and Knox, *Delta Force*, pp. 229–31.

10. Pete Szilagyi, "Always a Soldier at Heart," *Austin* (Texas) *American Statesman*, 8 November 1981, pp. A1, A13 (interview with Colonel Beckwith).

11. Holloway Report, p. 16, describes Colonel Kyle's role. *Aviation Week*, 12 May 1980, p. 16, reports that Marine Col. Charles H. Pitman was a leader, Lt. Col. E. R. Seiffert was the helo flight leader, and Maj. John T. Carney was the chief of the control team at Desert One. Holloway Report, p. 51, uses the title "Deputy Commander for Helicopter Forces" in a clear reference to Pitman.

12. Holloway Report, p. 21, comments on the lack of a "murder board."

13. Ibid., pp. 16–20, 60.

14. Ibid., pp. 19, 39, 59.

15. Ibid., p. 20; and Beckwith and Knox, *Delta Force*, pp. 196, 199–200, 220–23.

16. David C. Martin, "Inside the Rescue Mission," *Newsweek*, 12 July 1982, pp. 16–22; Carter, *Keeping Faith*, p. 509; and Beckwith and Knox, *Delta Force*, p. 264.

17. Holloway Report, pp. 27–28. Colonel Beckwith revealed that Farsi-speaking men were in his group (see his Pentagon press conference transcript [photocopy], 1 May 1980, p. 2; and Beckwith and Knox, *Delta Force*, pp. 260, 261, 263).

18. Letter from R. G. H. Carroll of Sikorsky Aircraft, dated 19 July 1982, to author; and Holloway Report, pp. 32–34. The characteristics of the helicopter are described in *Jane's All the World's Aircraft* (London: Jane's Publishing Co., 1981), pp. 460–61; and Norman Polmar et al., eds., *World Combat Aircraft Directory* (New York: Doubleday, 1976), pp. 352–53.

19. Donald C. Fine, "Rescue Helicopters Drawn from Fleet," *Aviation Week*, 5 May 1980, pp. 24–25; see also *Armed Forces Journal International*, June 1980, p. 16.

20. Holloway Report, pp. 33–34.

21. Ibid.

22. Holloway Report, pp. 27–28, 33–34; Richard Gabriel, "Military Displays Bad Flaws," *Washington Star*, 1 February 1981, pp. G7, G10; "Readiness Rate of RH-53 Key Issue," *Aviation Week*, 5 May 1980; Alexander Scott, "The Lessons of the Iranian Raid for American Military Policy," *Armed Forces Journal International*, June 1980, pp. 26–32, 73; Beckwith and Knox, *Delta Force*, pp. 232–33; and Beckwith's interview with Bill Small, 5 November 1983, on radio station KCBS program "Round Table," San Francisco.

23. Brzezinski, "The Failed Mission," p. 63.

24. Jay Lewis, "Charles Beckwith," *Dallas Times Herald*, Westwood Magazine section, 30 May 1982, p. 16. This article is an excellent profile of Colonel Beckwith.

25. Admiral Holloway in a talk at U.S. Naval Air Station, Alameda, Calif., on 6 October 1982; *Raleigh* (N.C.) *News and Observer*, 4 May 1982, pp. 1, 22; and Holloway Report, p. 15.

26. Holloway Report, pp. 35–36.

Chapter 3

1. *Wall Street Journal*, 12 March 1981, p. 22; and Brzezinski, "The Failed Mission," p. 29. For a detailed account of the SonTay raid, see Benjamin F. Schemmer, *The Raid* (New York, Harper & Row, 1976).

2. *U.S. News & World Report*, 14 April 1980, p. 19. See Steven R. Weisman, "For America, a Painful Reawakening," *New York Times Magazine*, 17 May 1981, p. 114–20, for an analysis of U.S. public opinion and the role of television in "fueling the rage of Americans." *Time*, 14 April 1980, p. 25; and Jordan, *Crisis*, pp. 240–52, give a White House view of U.S. public opinion.

3. Brzezinski, "The Failed Mission," pp. 29–30, Carter, *Keeping Faith*, pp. 501, 504; *Time*, 18 October 1982, p. 57; Vance, *Hard Choices*, pp. 408–9; and Beckwith and Knox, *Delta Force*, pp. 230, 235–36.

4. Holloway Report, pp. vi, 7, 8, 49–50; and Armstrong, Wilson, and Woodward, "Debate Rekindles on Failed Iran Raid," pp. A1, A14.

5. See State Department *Bulletin*, May 1980, p. 7, for an account of Carter's press conference, 10 April 1980; Carter, *Keeping Faith*, pp. 506–8; and *Time*, 18 October 1982, p. 57.

6. Brzezinski, "The Failed Mission," p. 62.

7. Ibid., 63.

8. Ibid.; and Carter, *Keeping Faith*, pp. 507–13. See also *New York Times*, 28 April 1980, p. A11; and Vance, *Hard Choices*, pp. 409–10. Jordan, *Crisis*, pp. 252–54, gives a verbatim account of Vance's dissent.

9. Terence Smith, "Putting the Hostages' Lives First," *New York Times Magazine*, 17 May 1981, Section 4, p. 100.

10. Holloway Report, p. 6; David R. Griffiths, "Readiness Rate of RH-53 Key Issue," *Aviation Week*, 5 May 1980, p. 22, 12 May 1980, p. 17; and Jones Report, p. 9.

11. Admiral Thomas Hayward, chief of naval operations, in speech to Society of American Naval Engineers, Washington, 1 May 1980, printed in *Congressional Record*, 6 May 1980, p. H-E2229; Jones Report, pp. 9–10; *Aviation Week*, 12 May 1980, p. 17; *Washington Post*, 25 August 1980, p. A27; and Assistant Defense Secretary Thomas Ross, News Briefing, 1 May 1980, p. 7 (photocopy).

12. Beckwith and Knox, *Delta Force*, p. 285.

13. Joel Larus, "Diego Garcia: Political Clouds over Vital U.S. Base," *Strategic Review*, Winter 1982, p. 51, describes Mrs. Thatcher's handling of the matter. Carter, *Keeping Faith*, p. 512; and Squadron Leader J. Clementson, RAF, in "Diego Garcia," *RUSI* (Journal of the Royal United Services Institute for Defence Studies), June 1981, p. 37, states that the C-130s of the support group used Diego Garcia as a base.

14. Brzezinski, "The Failed Mission," pp. 63–64; Carter, *Keeping Faith*, pp. 507–8; and Jordan, *Crisis*, pp. 262–64, all describe the meeting. See also Beckwith and Knox, *Delta Force*, pp. 5–8. For the hostages' evaluation of their captors, see McFadden, *No Hiding Place*, pp. 119–25.

15. Brzezinski, "The Failed Mission," pp. 63–64. For Admiral Moorer's remarks, see *Kansas City Star*, 4 May 1980, p. 5A.

16. British Broadcasting Corporation television program "Panorama," 26 July 1982, tape of Beckwith interview, held by Navy Department. See also David Martin, "Inside the Rescue Mission," pp. 19–20; and Beckwith and Knox, *Delta Force*, pp. 7–9, 258.

Chapter 4

1. Carter, *Keeping Faith*, p. 508; and *Time*, 18 October 1982, p. 57.

2. BBC television program "Panorama." Carter, *Keeping Faith*, p. 516, states that he was ready to send in carrier aircraft to protect the crew of any abandoned helicopter. See also Beckwith and Knox, *Delta Force*, pp. 255–56, 261.

3. *Washington Post*, 25 April 1982, p. 15, contains an account by George C. Wilson; *Newsweek*, 12 July 1982, pp. 18–22; *Aviation Week*, 5 May 1980, p. 23. Beckwith confirms the *Post* story in *Delta Force*, p. 265, concerning his team's battle dress; see pp. 6, 200–202 for weaponry carried and mission of C-130 gunships.

4. Martin, "Inside the Rescue Mission," p. 19; and Beckwith and Knox, *Delta Force*, pp. 199, 264; Logan Fitch with George Feifer, "Death at Desert One," *Penthouse*, March 1984, pp. 67, 173.

5. Jones Report, pp. 11–13; *Aviation Week*, 5 May 1980, p. 25, 19 May 1980, pp. 91–94; Holloway Report, p. 9; and L. Edgar Prina in *Sea Power*, June 1980, pp. 17–19.

6. Jones Report, pp. 6, 15; and Holloway Report, pp. 30–31, 44–46. The details on helo 2's hydraulic system are given in "CH-53A/D NATOPS Flight Manual."

7. Jones Report, p. 15; *Newsweek*, 12 July 1982, pp. 18–20; and Holloway Report, pp. 9–10, 38.

8. Holloway Report, pp. 38–39, states "The AWS [Air Weather Service] team had little or no interface with the mission pilots—they were both exclusively compartmented."

9. Jones Report, pp. 12–13; Holloway Report, pp. 40–41; and Martin, "New Light on the Rescue Mission," pp. 18–20.

10. Holloway Report, pp. 30, 45, 46, 51; and Beckwith and Knox, *Delta Force*, p. 283.

11. Holloway Report, pp. 30, 45, 51; and Jones Report, pp. 15–16; sanitized log of *Nimitz* provided by Navy Department.

12. Beckwith Pentagon Press Conference, 1 May 1980, pp. 4–5; and Holloway Report, p. 30.

13. Holloway Report, pp. 29–31, 40–41.

14. Ibid., pp. 45–48.

15. Ibid., pp. 39.

16. Ibid., pp. 40–43.

17. Ibid.

Chapter 5

1. Jones Report, p. 18; and Holloway Report, p. 50. *Newsweek*, 12 July 1982, p. 19, states that there were eight Iranians with Beckwith; Carter, *Keeping Faith*, p. 519, reports that he met five Iranian mission members after the operation.

2. Beckwith and Knox, *Delta Force*, p. 269.

3. "The Iran Raid," *Gung-Ho*, January 1983, p. 30; Colonel Beckwith, Pentagon Press Conference, p. 3; Carter, *Keeping Faith*, pp. 514–18, presents a timetable of the actual operation with Carter's comments. See also Holloway Report, pp. 50–52; and Beckwith and Knox, *Delta Force*, pp. 209, 270, 271, 275.

4. Holloway Report, pp. 16, 50, 51, 53. See also Maj. Robert L. Earl, USMC, "A Matter of Principle," U.S. Naval Institute *Proceedings*, February 1983, p. 35; and Beckwith and Knox, *Delta Force*, p. 248.

5. Information on C-130 start-up obtained from an individual close to the operation. See also Beckwith and Knox, *Delta Force*, pp. 232, 275.

6. *Newsweek*, 12 July 1982, p. 22; and Colonel Beckwith, Pentagon Press Conference, p. 5.

7. Holloway Report, pp. 45, 51; and Jones Report, p. 17.

8. *New York Times*, 2 May 1982, pp. 1, 22; and *Newsweek*, 12 July 1982, p. 22. The Holloway Report, p. 8, makes clear that General Vaught had decided on a minimum of six helicopters. Jordan, *Crisis*, pp. 280–81, presents Beckwith's account of the scene at Desert One.

9. General Jones, News Conference, Pentagon, 29 April 1980, p. 1; Carter, *Keeping Faith*, p. 516; and Beckwith and Knox, *Delta Force*, p. 277.

10. Brzezinski, "The Failed Mission," pp. 72–79; Carter, *Keeping Faith*, pp. 515–16; Jordan, *Crisis*, p. 261, quotes Beckwith to the effect that in December 1969, he and Generals Vaught and Gast agreed on six helos as a minimum; Beckwith and Knox, *Delta Force*, pp. 277–79. *Delta Force*, on pp. 264–65, describes Beckwith's changes in the assault plan at Qena, Egypt.

11. Jones Report, pp. 20–22; *New York Times*, 28 April 1980, p. A10, 2 May 1980, p. A12, and 5 May 1980, P. A3; Colonel Beckwith, Pentagon Press Conference, 1 May 1980, pp. 8–9; "Rescue Pilot Tells How Fiery Horror Split the Night," *Raleigh* (N.C.) *News and Observer*, 4 May 1980, pp. 1, 22, contains an eyewitness account by the unnamed marine pilot of helicopter 4; Drew Middleton, "Going the Military Route," in McFadden, *No Hiding Place*, pp. 217–18; and Beckwith and Knox, *Delta Force*, p. 279.

12. Holloway Report, p. 51.

13. Jones Report, p. 18; "The Iran Raid," *Gung-Ho*, p. 30. See also eyewitness account, *Raleigh* (N.C.) *News and Observer*, 4 May 1980, p. 22.

14. Colonel Beckwith, Pentagon Press Conference, 1 May 1980, p. 8; Holloway Report, p. 53; and Beckwith and Knox, *Delta Force*, pp. 208–81.

15. Holloway Report, pp. 53–54; Jones Report, p. 22; *Newsweek*, 30 June 1980, pp. 18–20; Carter, *Keeping Faith*, p. 513; and *New York Times*, 28 April 1980, p. A10, all describe the diagrams, maps, and photographs. See also Beckwith and Knox, *Delta Force*, pp. 279–83.

16. Carter, *Keeping Faith*, pp. 517–18. Martin, "Inside the Rescue Mission," p. 25, states that Major Meadows left Tehran on a commercial flight to Ankara and that all other agents got out safely. See also *Time*, 18 October 1982, p. 62; Brzezinski, "The Failed Mission," p. 78; *Newsweek*, 26 May 1980, p. 47; and *Time*, 12 May 1980, p. 33. For Carter's request for Kennedy's statement after the Bay of Pigs, see *Time*, 5 May 1980, p. 19; and Beckwith and Knox, *Delta Force*, pp. 279–83.

Chapter 6

1. *New York Times*, 28 April 1980, p. 11; Carter's letter is in White House press release (photocopy) dated 25 April 1982, 7 A.M. EST. His message to all U.S. embassies of 25 April 1980 provided by Congressional Research Service of Library of Congress. See also *Aviation Week*, 19 May 1980, pp. 91–94; and Carter, *Keeping Faith*, pp. 513–14. For an analysis of

rescue mission in terms of international law, see Congressional Research Study, "Iran: Consequences of the Abortive Attempt to Rescue the American Hostages," (photocopy), 2 May 1980, pp. 7–8.

2. *Newsweek*, 5 May 1980, p. 24; *U.S. News & World Report*, 12 May 1980, p. 25. On the navy's manpower shortage, see Paul B. Ryan, *First Line of Defense*, pp. 175–76; and Gen. David C. Jones, news conference, 29 April 1980, pp. 1–3. See also James R. Schlesinger, "Some Lessons of Iran," *New York Times*, 6 May 1980, p. A27.

3. *Aerospace Daily*, 29 April 1980, p. 33.

4. Admiral Hayward, speech to Society of Naval Engineers, Washington, D.C., 1 May 1980, printed in *Congressional Record*, 6 May 1980, pp. H-E2229-30. Oddly enough, the *New York Times* ignored Hayward's speech and the *Washington Post* gave it only a few paragraphs. See also Lt. Col. Richard F. Braucr, USAF, "Planning Imperatives Applicable to Hostage Rescue Operations," (Carlisle Barracks, PA: U.S. Army War College, 1984), p. 17 and Benjamin F. Schemmer, *The Raid* (New York: Harper and Row, 1976), p. 237.

5. *Newsweek*, 5 May 1980, p. 24, contains result of Gallup poll in which respondents approved, by ratio of four to one, Carter's decision to send in the rescue force; *Business Week*, 12 May 1980, p. 7. See also "A Grim Postmortem Begins," *Newsweek*, 12 May 1980, pp. 29–32.

6. "The Iranian Debacle," *National Review*, 16 May 1980, p. 574.

7. *Time*, 5 May 1980, p. 31, 12 May 1980, p. 32; William Shawcross, "The President Is Dropped by His Pilot," *New Statesman* (London), 2 May 1980, p. 658; George Will, *Washington Post*, 1 May 1980, p. A19; and *New York Times*, 27 April 1980, p. N22, 26 April 1980, p. 26, 1 May 1980, p. 31.

8. Edward N. Luttwak, "The Decline of American Military Leadership," *Parameters*, Journal of Army War College, December 1980, p. 86.

9. *U.S. News & World Report*, 5 May 1980, pp. 13, 21–22, 40–41, 12 May 1980, pp. 22–23; *New Statesman*, 2 May 1980, p. 654; *New York Times*, 26 April 1980, p. 10; *Business Week*, 12 May 1980, p. 27; "Iran," Congressional Research Service, pp. 16–17; *Time*, 5 May 1980, pp. 26, 30–31; and Department of State *Bulletin*, January 1980, pp. E, F, G, H.

10. "Iran," Congressional Research Service, p. 15. Soviet Foreign Minister Andrei Gromyko vented his "indignation over U.S. intrusion on Iranian territory"; see *National Review*, 16 May 1980, p. 572; and *Time*, 5 May 1980, pp. 26, 31.

11. Queen, *Inside and Out*, pp. 179–82; Pierre Salinger, *America Held Hostage* (Garden City, N.Y.: Doubleday, 1981), p. 239; and "The Failed Rescue," *Newsweek*, 9 February 1981, pp. 38–39.

12. *New York Times*, 6 May 1980, p. 1, reported Carter had ruled out future use of force. See also George C. Wilson, "Pentagon Scrubbed a Second Iranian Rescue Plan as Too Dangerous," *Washington Post*, 25 January

1981, p. 19; and Brzezinski, "The Failed Mission," p. 79. Middleton, "Going the Military Route," reports a second rescue plan for which training took place on the western desert. Two years after the raid, Carter told journalist Barbara Walters that he had been "absolutely" prepared to strike Iran if any one of the hostages was injured or killed by their guards (see *San Francisco Chronicle*, 15 October 1982, p. 17). One military source who cannot be identified said that a secret force was ready to rescue the hostages right up to the day the prisoners were returned to freedom.

13. Defense Secretary Harold Brown, news conference, 25 April 1980 (photocopy), 25 April 1980, pp. 1–2, 4, 5, 6.

14. Colonel Beckwith on BBC television program "Panorama," 26 July 1982.

15. Secretary Harold Brown and Gen. David C. Jones, news conference, 29 April 1980, pp. 2, 5; and Beckwith and Knox, *Delta Force*, pp. 288–90, 292.

16. Beckwith, Pentagon Press Conference, 1 May 1980, photocopy provided by Pentagon's Public Affairs Office. See also *New York Times*, 2 May 1980, pp. A1–A12.

17. Library of Congress, Congressional Research Service, *The Iran Hostage Crisis*, Report DS-320 (Washington, D.C.: Government Printing Office, May 1981), pp. 11–25. Deputy Secretary of State Warren Christopher and Algerian Foreign Minister Mohammed Ben Yahia signed the accord on 19 January 1980. For a summary, see *San Francisco Chronicle*, 21 January 1980, p. 19. See also State Department, Bureau of Public Affairs, "Hostage Agreements Transmitted to Congress," dated 12 March 1981.

Chapter 7

1. The review group's terms of reference are given on pp. 63–64 in the Holloway Report. In the foreword to the report, Admiral Holloway states that because of the need of the American public to have as many details as possible, a declassified version of the document was made available. The issues and findings in the latter were retained in as close a form as possible to the classified version, and the recommendations remained virtually unchanged, he said, in an interview with the author.

2. Biographical sketches of the members appear on pp. 1–3 and 66–78 of the Holloway Report.

3. Remarks to the Association of Naval Aviation at Naval Air Station, Alameda, Calif., 6 October 1982.

4. Holloway Report, pp. v, 12, 57–60.

5. Ibid., pp. 3–4.

6. Ibid., pp. 11–12, 63–64.

7. Ibid., pp. vi, 13–14.

8. Ibid., pp. 17–18, 60.

9. Ibid., see forwarding statement attached to report, and p. 57.

10. Ibid. These points are emphasized on pp. 13–14, 17, 58. The review group acknowledged that its differences with Vaught's OPSEC practices "epitomize the advantage of hindsight." The group also was reluctant to criticize the OPSEC rules because of the importance of secrecy (essential for surprise).

11. Ibid., pp. 15, 23–26, 59.

12. Ibid., pp. 25–26.

13. Ibid., pp. v, 15–18, 50–52, 58.

14. Ibid., pp. 16, 18, 25–26, 59.

15. Ibid., pp. iv, 11–12, 23; and Colonel Beckwith's interview on BBC program "Panorama."

16. Holloway Report, pp. v, 16.

17. Ibid., pp. vi, 16, 50, 51.

18. Jones Report, p. 2; Holloway Report, pp. 23, 50–51, 59. In his BBC "Panorama" interview, Admiral Holloway emphasized that "every hour or so a Soviet satellite goes overhead [scanning the American western desert]." He added that the concern for secrecy "was very valid, that had the Russians detected the movement of [U.S.] forces in a very definable pattern such as that of a remote area then the Iranians would have been tipped off." Yet the Holloway Report, p. 59, states that if OPSEC militated against full-scale rehearsal, "the possible security disadvantages of such a rehearsal seem to be outweighed by the advantages to be gained."

19. Holloway Report, pp. vi, 48, 51, 52, 59.

20. Ibid., pp. 53–55; and Beckwith and Knox, *Delta Force*, p. 283.

21. Holloway Report, pp. 29, 31, 47, 48.

22. Ibid., pp. vi, 61, 62.

Chapter 8

1. Admiral Holloway, speech at Alameda, Calif., 6 October 1982.

2. "Priest Stirred Persian Mobs to Kill Imbrie by Accusing Him of Poisoning Sacred Well," *New York Times*, 24 August 1924, p. 1.

3. Steven R. Weisman, "For America, a Painful Reawakening," in McFadden, *No Hiding Place*, p. 230. Daniel Yankelovich and Larry Kaagan in "Assertive America," *Foreign Affairs* 59 (1981), p. 697, state that in a 14 May 1980 poll for *Time*, 65 percent of the public agreed that the capture of the hostages and the handling of crisis had lowered U.S. prestige. A *New York Times*/CBS poll published 25 June 1980, pp. 1, 3, found only 20 percent of the public approved Carter's conduct of foreign policy.

4. McFadden, *No Hiding Place*, pp. 98–100, 141–42, describe in detail the reaction of the hostages.

5. Videotape of BBC's program, "Panorama."

6. Holloway Report, pp. 35–36.

7. *Newsweek*, 12 July 1982, p. 22; and Beckwith and Knox, *Delta Force*, pp. 276, 283.

8. Richard A. Gabriel, "A Commando Operation That Was Wrong from the Start," *Canadian Defense Quarterly*, Winter 1980–81, pp. 9–10.

9. BBC television program "Panorama." Colonel Beckwith was convinced that there were people in Washington who wanted all four services involved (Lewis, "Charles Beckwith," p. 16; and Beckwith and Knox, *Delta Force*, p. 225).

10. Brzezinski, "The Failed Mission," p. 79. A White House official reportedly agreed, asking if "we've psyched ourselves into putting too much faith in our machines" (*Business Week*, 12 May 1980, p. 28).

11. Armstrong, Wilson, and Woodward, "Debate Rekindles on Failed Iran Raid," pp. A1, A14.

12. Letter to author, 16 August 1983.

Chapter 9

1. The Bay of Pigs affair is covered in Mario Lazo, *Dagger in the Heart: American Foreign Policy Failures in Cuba* (New York: Twin Circle Publishing Co., 1968), and Peter Wyden, *Bay of Pigs: The Untold Story* (New York: Simon and Schuster, 1979).

2. For comments on the relationship between the White House and the JCS, see "Official Inside Story of the Cuba Invasion," *U.S. News & World Report*, 13 August 1979, pp. 79–83; and Arthur Krock, *In the Nation, 1932–1966* (New York: McGraw-Hill, 1967), pp. 321–25.

3. The *Pueblo* capture is well covered in Trevor Armbrister, *A Matter of Accountability: The True Story of the Pueblo Affair* (New York: Coward-McCann, 1970). See also Paul B. Ryan, *First Line of Defense: The U.S. Navy since 1945* (Stanford: Hoover Institution Press, 1981), pp. 43–45; and *Bucher: My Story* (New York: Doubleday, 1970), written by Commander Lloyd M. Bucher, who commanded the *Pueblo*, and Mark Rascovich, a professional writer.

4. For details of the *Mayaguez* rescue as told by a White House staff member, see Robert T. Hartmann, *Palace Politics: An Inside Account of the Ford Years* (New York: McGraw-Hill, 1980), pp. 327–29. "Mayday for the *Mayaguez*," U.S. Naval Institute *Proceedings*, November 1978, pp. 93–111, is a detailed description of the rescue as told by a patrol plane squadron commander, two destroyer skippers, a marine captain, and a marine battalion operations officer. The ordeal of the *Mayaguez* crew is told in Roy Rowen, *The Four Days of Mayaguez* (New York, Norton, 1975).

5. Hugh Sidey, "*Mayaguez* Reconsidered," Washington Star, 11 May 1980, p. F3.

6. Joint Chiefs of Staff, *Military Posture for FY 1983* (Washington, D.C.: Government Printing Office, 1982), p. 99. See also "U.S. Reviving Guerrilla War Forces," *San Francisco Chronicle*, 19 July 1982, pp. 1, 14.

7. After the Desert One episode, the press reported that the JCS had created a joint-service staff to develop plans for future rescue missions and to train special forces to carry out these operations (*San Francisco Chronicle*, 15 February 1981, p. 20A). Two years later the army announced plans to expand its special forces from 3,600 to 4,800 men (*San Francisco Chronicle*, 19 July 1982, p. 1, 24 February 1983, p. 14).

8. Lieut. General John S. Pustay, USAF (Ret.), "The Problem is Systemic," *Armed Forces Journal International*, February 1984, pp. 28–29.

Epilogue

1. Timothy Ashby, "Grenada: Soviet Stepping Stone," Naval Institute *Proceedings*, December 1983, pp. 30–35; *U.S. News & World Report*, 31 October 1983, p. 35; and *Grenada, A Preliminary Report*, a forty-three page summary, released by the Departments of State and Defense, 16 December 1983.

2. *Gist* (Department of State monthly report), January 1984, p. 2, contains a summary of the Grenada action. See Congressman Richard Cheney's description of the plight of the U.S. medical students, *Washington Post*, 14 November 1983, p. A17; President Reagan's speech, 27 April 1983, to the Congress: Timothy Ashby, "Grenada: Threat to America's Caribbean Oil Routes," *National Defense*, May–June 1981, pp. 52–54; *Time*, 31 October 1983, p. 78.

3. *Gist*, p. 1.

4. *Time*, 7 November 1983, p. 26; 21 November 1983, p. 17; 28 November 1983, p. 21.

5. Conversations with U.S. naval officers associated with the operation; Gerald F. Seib, "No More 'Micromanagement' of the Military," *Wall Street Journal*, 8 November 1983, p. 24.

6. For Schlesinger's article, see *Wall Street Journal*, 9 November 1983, p. 3. See also *New York Times*, 26 October 1983, p. A26. For U.S. public opinion surveys and comment, see *Wall Street Journal*, 3 November 1983, p. 25; 11 November 1983, p. 1; *Time*, 14 November 1983, p. 19; 21 November 1983, p. 16. For on-the-scene evaluations of the Grenada mission by Congressmen Richard Cheney (R, Wyo.) and William S. Broomfield (R, Mich.), see *Washington Post*, 14 November 1983, p. A17; *Wall Street Journal*, 15 November 1983, pp. 1, 21.

7. *Gist*, p. 1; *Time*, 7 November 1983, p. 26.

8. John J. Fialka, "In Battle for Grenada, Commando Mission Didn't Go as Planned," *Wall Street Journal*, 15 November 1983, pp. 1, 21; Benjamin E. Schemmer, "Grenada Highlights One of DOD's Major C³ Problems, But Increased Funding Is Bringing Solutions," *Armed Forces Journal International*, February 1984, pp. 51–52. ("C³" is a Pentagon symbol for Command, Control, and Communications.)

9. "U.S. Policy toward the Persian Gulf" (Current Policy No. 390), a four-page pamphlet, dated 10 May 1982, and issued by the Department of State, describes U.S. interest in maintaining the integrity of Middle East nations. Reagan's statement is quoted in the *San Francisco Sunday Examiner* and *Chronicle*, 11 December 1983, p. A18. See also Rick Jaroslovsky and Albert R. Hunt, "Reagan Toughens Line on Troops in Lebanon and Chides His Critics," *Wall Street Journal*, 3 February 1984, pp. 1, 7; *U.S. News & World Report*, 9 January 1984, p. 21.

10. The 141-page *Report of the DOD Commission on Beirut International Airport Terrorist Act, October 23, 1983*, dated 20 December 1983, was released to the press in typescript. I have drawn extensively from this report, hereafter referred to as the Long Commission report. See also Philip Taubman and Joel Brinkley, "The Marine Tragedy: An Inquiry Into Causes and Responsibility," *New York Times*, 11 December 1983, pp. 15–18. See also "Reagan Says He Shares Blame for Death of Marines in Beirut," *San Francisco Sunday Examiner & Chronicle*, 25 December 1983, p. 8.

11. Long Commission report, pp. 37–38, 40–41, 47–49. The commission suggested that Defense Secretary Caspar Weinberger "take whatever administrative or disciplinary action he deems appropriate." Although Navy Secretary John Lehman reportedly recommended that military officers be reprimanded for command failures through the issuance of "disciplinary letters," it was not known what recommendations were made, respectively, by the secretaries of the army and air force. See *San Francisco Chronicle*, 10 January 1984, p. 11.

12. Ibid., pp. 54–46.

13. Ibid., pp. 63–66.

14. Ibid., pp. 6–7.

15. Deborah M. Kyle, "Stronger Chairman/JCS System Sought by House Investigations Subcommittee Bill," *Armed Forces Journal International*, September 1983, pp. 14, 117. For an analysis of the proposed military command system headed by the chairman of the JCS, see former Defense Secretary James R. Schlesinger, "Reorganizing the Joint Chiefs," *Wall Street Journal*, 8 February 1984, p. 24. An opposing view is given by Lt. Gen. Victor II. Krulak, USMC (Ret.), *Organization for National Security: A Study* (Washington, D.C.: United States Strategic Institute, 1983).

Glossary of Military Terms

Abort   Failure to accomplish a mission for any reason other than enemy action. It may occur at any point from initiation of operation to destination.

Alert   Readiness for action, defense, or protection. A warning signal of danger. To forewarn. To prepare for action. The period of time during which troops stand by in response to an alarm.

Austere   As used by the services, a term meaning "no extras." Bare essentials, in equipment.

Bird, helo   Helicopter. See chopper, helo.

Blivet   Fuel bladder stowed internally in cargo aircraft.

C-130   A large troop and cargo transport aircraft with turboprop engines. Built by Lockheed. Known as the Hercules.

Call sign   Any combination of characters or words which identifies a command or unit; used to establish and maintain communications.

Chain of command   The succession of commanders from a superior to a subordinate through which command is exercised.

Chopper, helo   Helicopter. See Bird, helo.

Classified document   Official information which requires protection against unauthorized disclosure and which has been so designated.

Combat control team   A team of specially trained personnel who can be airdropped or landed to advise on landing requirements or to provide local air control for aircraft.

Command   Authority vested in an individual for the direction, coordination, and control of military forces. An order to bring about a particular action. A unit, an organization, or an area under the command of one individual.

Command and control   The exercise of authority and direction by a commander over assigned forces in the accomplishment of his mission.

Command post   A unit's headquarters where the commander and his staff carry out their activities.

Commando   A military unit of specially trained shock troops organized for hit-and-run raids into hostile territory to sabotage installations, to obtain information, or to seize personnel. A member of the unit.

Compartmentation   Establishment and management of an organization so that information on one component is made available to another component only to the extent required for the performance of assigned duties.

Compatibility   The capability of two or more items or equipments to function in the same system or environment without mutual interference, as a helicopter in a ship.

Contingency plan   A plan for major contingencies that can be reasonably anticipated.

Control   Authority over the operations or activities of subordinate organizations.

Counterinsurgency   Those military, paramilitary, political, psychological, and civic actions taken to defeat subversive insurgency.

Critique   A critical discussion of a mission or exercise just performed, setting forth mistakes and successes.

D-day   The unnamed day on which a particular operation commences or is to commence.

Dead reckoning (from ded. [deduced] reckoning)   A method used in estimating the position of an aircraft or ship by taking in account: the last known position, elapsed time, speed, course steered, and influence of wind or current.

Delta Force   An elite body of Green Berets trained for special operations, particularly of a covert nature.

Desert One   A salt flat 250 miles southeast of Tehran in the area known as Dasht-e-Kavr. This spot served as a rendezvous for the helicopters and C-130s on the first leg of the proposed assault.

Desert Two   A remote spot in the mountains some fifty miles from Tehran.

Destruct (missile)   Intentional destruction of a missile, a vehicle, classified material, or equipment for safety, to avoid compromise or for any other reason.

Doctrine   Fundamental principles by which the military forces guide their actions in support of national objectives. It is authoritative but requires judgment in application.

Electronic intelligence (ELINT)   Technical and intelligence information derived from foreign, noncommunications, electronic-magnetic radiations emanating from (usually unfriendly) sources.

Electronic warfare (EW)   Military action in the use of electromagnetic energy against an enemy's use of the electromagnetic spectrum. ER includes jamming and electronic deception.

Evasion and escape   The procedures by which individuals are enabled to emerge from hostile areas to safety. Popularly known as E and E.

Green Beret   A member of the elite special forces, trained to conduct unconventional warfare on covert missions.

Helicopter assault force   A task organization combining helicopters, supporting units, and helicopter-borne troop units for use in helicopter-borne assault operations.

Helo   Helicopter. See chopper, bird.

Hercules   See C-130.

Hostage   A person held as a pledge that certain terms or agreements will be kept. (The taking of hostages is forbidden under the Geneva Conventions of 1949.)

Interface   A boundary or point common to two or more command and control systems or other entities at which information is passed. Frequently used loosely to mean "communicate."

J-2   An abbreviation for a Joint Staff Intelligence officer and his staff.

JCS   See Joint Chiefs of Staff.

Joint Chiefs of Staff (JCS)   The principal military advisors to the president, the National Security Council, and the secretary of defense. The members are chiefs of staff of the army and air force; the chief of naval operations; and the commandant of the marine corps. The president appoints a fifth four-star officer to serve as chairman.

Logistics   The science of planning and carrying out the movement and maintenance of forces.

MEDEVAC   Medical air evacuation by specially fitted aircraft.

Medic   Medical officer. Anyone connected with the medical service.

MiG   A designation for certain Russian fighter-aircraft designed by Mikoyan and Gurevich.

Mission   The task, together with its purpose, assigned to a commander for attaining an objective.

Murder board   Term used to describe a group of individuals whose function is to make an independent assessment of a proposed operation. The members do not participate in the actual planning.

National command authorities   The president and the secretary of defense or their duly deputized alternates or successors.

National intelligence surveys   Basic intelligence studies produced on a coordinated interdepartmental basis on a foreign country or other area.

National objectives   Those fundamental aims, goals, or purposes of a nation—as opposed to the means for seeking these ends.

Operation order   A formal statement or order issued by a commander for a combat operation or maneuver. It contains information on the situation, the mission, communications, weather predictions, and so forth and assigns specific tasks to subordinate units.

Operational control   The authority delegated to a commander to assign missions or tasks to subordinate commands, to deploy units, to reassign forces, and to retain operational or tactical control as necessary.

Operational readiness   The condition or state of training of a unit being readied to carry out the type of operation required by the mission.

Operations security (OPSEC)   The protection of military operations and activities resulting from the identification and subsequent elimination or control of indicators susceptible to hostile exploitation.

Radio silence   A condition existing when radio transmissions are stopped on some or all frequencies.

Ranger   A soldier trained in close-range fighting and raiding tactics. See commando.

Rendezvous   As a noun, a prearranged meeting at a given time and place from which to begin a phase of the operation. As a verb, to assemble, meet with others.

Pathfinder   An aircraft employed to guide other aircraft to a target. Also an aircraft used to carry special teams to set up navigational aids or target markers, which precede the main force to the landing zone, drop zone, or target.

Payload   The load, expressed in tons of cargo, gallons of fuel, or number of passengers, which a vehicle is designed to transport under specified conditions, in addition to its unladen weight.

Prisoner of war (POW)   According to the Geneva Convention of 1949, a military prisoner (or a member of other forces defined by the Convention) who is captured by an enemy during war.

Safe house   An innocent-appearing house or premises established for the purpose of conducting covert actions in relative security.

Sanitize   To revise a document so as to prevent identification of sources or of persons and places. Usually involves deletion of details.

Scenario   The outline plan of the actions to be undertaken during a projected exercise or maneuver.

Security   A condition which results from the establishment of measures which protect designated information, personnel, and equipment against hostile persons, acts, or influences.

Self-destruction equipment   Equipment that may be destroyed by a self-contained explosive. Secret equipment exposed to the danger of capture may be so rigged.

Signal intelligence (SIGINT)   Information comprising all intelligence to do with communications, electronics, and telemetry intelligence.

Signal security (SIGSEC)   A generic term which includes communications security and electronic security.

Sortie   A sudden attack made from a defensive position. An operational flight by one aircraft. To depart from a point or anchorage.

Special Forces   Military personnel with cross training in basic and specialized military skills, organized in small, multi-purpose groups. Their mission is to train other forces in guerrilla warfare and to conduct unconventional warfare operations.

Special operations   Secondary or supporting operations which may be adjuncts to other operations and for which no single service is assigned primary responsibility.

Staging base   A landing and takeoff area with minimum servicing, supply, and shelter, used for temporary occupancy of military aircraft and personnel in movement from one location to another.

Strike   An attack intended to inflict damage on, to seize, or to destroy an objective.

Task force   A temporary grouping of units under one commander for carrying out a specific operation or mission.

Terrain following radar (TFR)   A radar that scans surface of land ahead from aircraft to disclose irregularities of the terrain, thus enabling the plane to maintain a selected height above the ground.

Transition   The training given a pilot as he moves from the operation of one aircraft to another. Sometimes used as a verb.

Unconventional warfare   Military and paramilitary operations conducted in enemy-held, enemy-denied, or politically sensitive territory. It includes guerrilla warfare, evation and escape, sabotage, direct action missions of a covert, clandestine nature.

Visual flight rules (VFR)   Rules restricting the flying of aircraft under conditions of contact flying at specified minimum altitudes and limits of visibility.

Zulu time   Greenwich mean time (GMT), frequently used in military operations involving several time zones. If all participants use Zulu time, they will operate on a common time-schedule.

Bibliography

General Works

Beckwith, Charlie A., and Donald Knox. *Delta Force.* New York: Harcourt Brace Jovanovich, 1983.

Blakey, Scott. *Prisoner at War: The Survival of Commander Richard A. Stratton.* New York: Doubleday, Anchor Press, 1978.

Brzezinski, Zbigniew. *Power and Principle: Memoirs of the National Security Adviser, 1977–1981.* New York: Farrar, Straus & Giroux, 1983.

Carter, Jimmy. *Keeping Faith.* New York: Bantam Books, 1982.

Jordan, Hamilton. *Crisis: The Last Year of the Carter Presidency.* New York: G. P. Putnam's Sons, 1982.

Krulak, Victor H. *Organization for National Security: A Study.* Washington, D.C.: United States Strategic Institute, 1983.

Ledeen, Michael, and William Lewis. *Debacle: The American Failure in Iran.* New York: Alfred A. Knopf, 1981.

McFadden, Robert D., et al. *No Hiding Place.* New York: Times Books, 1981.

Queen, Richard, with Patricia Hass. *Inside and Out: Hostage To Iran, Hostage to Myself.* New York: G. P. Putnam's Sons, 1981.

Rubin, Barry. *Paved with Good Intentions: The American Experience and Iran.* New York: Oxford University Press, 1980.

Ryan, Paul B. *First Line of Defense: The U.S. Navy Since 1945.* Stanford: Hoover Institution Press, 1981.

Salinger, Pierre. *America Held Hostage.* Garden City, N.Y.: Doubleday, 1981.

Stempel, John D. *Inside the Iranian Revolution.* Bloomington: Indiana University Press, 1981.

Sullivan, William H. *Mission to Iran.* New York: W. W. Norton & Co., 1981.

Vance, Cyrus. *Hard Choices.* New York: Simon & Schuster, 1983.

Articles

Armstrong, Scott; George C. Wilson; and Bob Woodward. "Debate Rekindles on Failed Iran Raid." *Washington Post,* 25 April 1982, pp. A1, A14.

Brzezinski, Zbigniew. "The Failed Mission." *New York Times Magazine,* 18 April 1982, pp. 28–79.

Clementson, J. "Diego Garcia." *RUSI* (Journal of the Royal United Services Institute for Defence Studies), June 1981, pp. 33–39.

Drucker, Peter. "Getting Control of Corporate Staff Work." *Wall Street Journal,* 28 April 1982, p. 28.

Earl, Robert L. "A Matter of Principle." U.S. Naval Institute *Proceedings,* February 1983, pp. 30–36.

Fallows, James. "Zbig without Cy." *New Republic,* 10 May 1980.

Fialka, John. "Vaught's Leadership Raises Some Questions on Hill." *Washington Star,* 15 May 1980, p. A3.

Fine, Donald C. "Rescue Helicopters Drawn from Fleet." *Aviation Week and Space Technology.* 5 May 1980, pp. 24–25.

Gabriel, Richard A. "Military Displays Bad Flaws." *Washington Star,* 1 February 1981, pp. G7, G10.

———. "The U.S. Rescue Mission into Iran, April 1980." *Canadian Defence Quarterly,* Winter 1980–81, pp. 6–10.

"The Iran Raid: Operation Blue Light, an Air Crew Member's Story." *Gung-Ho,* January 1983, pp. 27–30.

Jones, David C. "Why the Joint Chief of Staff Must Change." *Armed Forces Journal International,* March 1982, pp. 62–72.

Larus, Joel. "Diego Garcia: Political Clouds over a Vital U.S. Base." *Strategic Review,* Winter 1981, p. 51.

Lewis, Jay. "Charles Beckwith." *Dallas Times Herald,* Westward Magazine section, 30 May 1982, p. 16.

Luttwak, Edward N. "The Decline of American Military Leadership." *Parameters*, Journal of Army War College, December 1980, pp. 82–88.

Martin, David C. "Inside the Rescue Mission." *Newsweek*, 12 July 1982, pp. 16–22.

———. "New Light on the Rescue Mission." *Newsweek*, 30 June 1981, pp. 18–20.

Melbourne, Roy M. "America and Iran in Perspective: 1953 and 1980." *Atlantic Community Quarterly*, Fall 1980, pp. 346–62.

Middleton, Drew. "Going the Military Route." In Robert D. McFadden et al., *No Hiding Place*. New York: Times Books, 1981, pp. 215–26.

Moore, Robin. "Desert One." *Oui*, July 1982, pp. 9–10, 115–16.

Schemmer, Benjamin F. "President Courage—and the April 1980 Iranian Rescue Mission." *Armed Forces Journal International*, May 1981, pp. 60–62.

Scott, Alexander. "The Lessons of the Iranian Raid for American Military Policy." *Armed Forces Journal International*, June 1980, pp. 26–32, 73.

Smith, Terence. "Putting the Hostages' Lives First." In Robert D. McFadden et al., *No Hiding Place*. New York: Times Books, 1981, pp. 189–214.

Sorley, Lewis, "Turbulence at the Top: Our Peripatetic Generals." *Army*, March 1981, pp. 14–24.

Stockdale, James B. "The Hostages as 'Extortionist-Theatre.'" *Washington Post*, 25 January 1981, pp. 6–7.

Szilagyi, Pete. "Always a Soldier at Heart." *Austin* (Texas) *American Statesman*, 8 November 1981, pp. A1, A13.

Webbe, Stephen. "Chorus of Retired Admirals and Generals: Make U.S. Forces Battle Ready." *Christian Science Monitor*, 31 December 1980, p. 6

Weisman, Steven R. "For America, a Painful Reawakening." *New York Times Magazine*, 17 May 1981, pp. 114–20.

Welch, Edward F. "The JCS: Life Begins at 40?" *Shipmate* (Journal of U.S. Naval Academy Alumni Association), July 1982, p. 3.

Wilson, George C. "Pentagon Scrubbed a Second Iranian Rescue Plan as Too Dangerous." *Washington Post*, 25 January 1981, p. 19.

Television Transcripts and Videotapes

Donahue, Phil. "The Phil Donahue Show," television program transcript 09282, 1982, available from Phil Donahue, P.O. Box 2111, Cincinnati, Ohio 45200.

"Panorama," British Broadcasting Corporation television program. Interview of Colonel Charlie Beckwith, 26 July 1982. Videotape held by U.S. Navy Department.

Government Documents

U.S. Defense Department. "Rescue Mission Report" [Holloway Report]. August 1980. (Typescript.)

U.S. Defense Department, Office of Secretary of Defense. Transcript of General Jones's News Conference, 29 April 1980. (Typescript.)

———. Transcript of Defense Secretary's News Conferences, 25 and 29 April 1980. (Typescript.)

———. Colonel Beckwith's Press Conference, Pentagon, 1 May 1980. (Typescript.)

U.S. Joint Chiefs of Staff. David C. Jones. "Report on Rescue Mission" [Jones Report]. Office of Chairman, Joint Chiefs of Staff, 6 May 1980. (Typescript.)

U.S. Library of Congress, Congressional Research Service. *The Iran Hostage Crisis.* Report DS-320. Washington, D.C.: Government Printing Office, May 1981.

———. "Iran: Consequences of the Abortive Attempt to Rescue American Hostages," 2 May 1980.

U.S. Navy Department. Sanitized log of USS *Nimitz*, 24–25 April 1980.

U.S. State Department *Bulletin*, January 1980. "President Carter's News Conference of November 28 [1979]."

———. March 1980. "President Carter's News Conference of 13 February [1980]."

———. May 1980. "President Carter's Address before the American Society of Newspaper Editors," 10 April 1980.

U.S. State Department, Bureau of Public Affairs. "Hostage Agreements Transmitted to Congress." Pamphlet. 12 March 1981.

Index